Atkins Diet

Cookbook

181 Easy and Delicious Recipes to Help You Lose Weight and Improve Your Health

Maggie Vega

Table of Contents

Introduction

What is the Atkins Diet?

It is basically a low-carbs diet termed as Atkins Diet after the name of the physician Dr. Robert C. Atkins who promoted it in the year 1972. He also wrote a book in the same year to guide people with the diet.

The Atkins diet allows minimum intake of the carbohydrates so that body's metabolism boosts which helps in the burning of body's fat to produce energy and body undergo a process of ketosis. Ketosis process starts with the lower insulin levels in the body causing the consumption and burning of the fats to generate ketone bodies. On contrary, consumption of higher carbohydrates increases blood sugar levels thus accumulation of the fats occurs.

Atkins diet promotes simple eating habits which reduces the appetite. Atkins diet foods are rich in fats and proteins thus longer duration of digestion is required which lowers the raise of hunger.

Formerly, the Atkins diet was considered unhealthy because of the high saturated fat intake but recent research has proved it harmless. In fact the high consumption of high fat diet like Atkins diet has shown tremendous health improvements like lowering the blood sugar levels, cholesterol levels, triglycerides and makes you tidy up to look smarter and fresh. The main reason that is most appealing to use this diet is that it is helpful in lowering done your appetite which vanishes with a little intake of calories.

The Atkins Diet Plan

The Atkins diet is usually split up into 4 different phases with each phase with different food items:

Induction phase (phase 1): This phase of the diet is quite tough as one has to intake less than 20 grams of carbs each day for 2 weeks. High proteins and fats are encouraged to eat with leaf green vegetables that contain low carbohydrates. These healthy weeks will start your weight loss.

Balancing Phase (phase 2): In this phase, try to create a equilibrium in your diet by slowly adding low-carb vegetables, more nuts, and a little amount of fruit back in your food.

1. Fine-Tuning Phase (phase 3): Seeing yourself near the required goal or optimum weight you want then slowly add more carbohydrates in the diet plan to slow down the further weight loss now.

2. Maintenance Phase (phase 4): Each as much carbs as much you can but keep it in mind that the body shouldn't regain the weight. Excess of everything is bad.

A number of people skip the induction phase and intake lots of fruits and vegetables at the beginning that can be effective too. Other do prefer induction phase to activate ketosis process which is low-carb keto diet.

Foods for Atkins Diet:

People usually get confused what should be eating during the diet and what should not... an outlines of food is listed below:

Prohibited food:

Try to avoid the mentioned food items while you are on the Atkins diet plan:

Grains: Spelt, rye, Wheat, barley, rice.

Sugar: Fruit juices, cakes, Soft drinks, candy, ice cream, etc

Vegetable Oils: Soybean oil, cottonseed oil, corn oil, canola oil and many others.

Low-Fat Foods: foods those are rich in sugar content.

Trans Fats: The tin pack things with mentioning of hydrogenated ingredients on the list.

High-Carb Fruits: Apples, oranges, pears, bananas, grapes (while in induction

phase).

Starches: Sweet potatoes, Potatoes (for induction phase only).

High-Carb Vegetables: Turnips, Carrots, etc (for induction only).

Legumes: Lentils, chickpeas, beans.

Beneficial Food items:

Healthy food items like the following should be in your menu for the Atkins diet Seafood and Fatty Fish: Trout, Salmon, sardines, etc.

Meats: Lamb, chicken, Beef, pork, bacon and others.

Eggs: Eggs are rich in Omega-3.

Healthy Fats: Coconut oil, avocado oil and extra virgin olive oil.

Full-Fat Dairy: Butter, full-fat yoghurt, cheese, cream.

Low-Carb Vegetables: Spinach, broccoli, Kale, asparagus and others alike.

Nuts and Seeds: Macadamia nuts, sunflower seeds, almonds, walnuts, etc.

Breakfast

1. SPINACH CHICKEN PARMESAN

Ingredients:

- 1/3 cup grated Parmesan cheese
- 1/4 teaspoon Italian seasoning
- 6 skinless, boneless chicken breasts
- 1 tablespoon butter
- 1 tablespoon all-purpose flour
- 1/2 cup skim milk
- 1/2 (10 ounce) package frozen chopped spinach, thawed and drained

- 1 tablespoon chopped pimento peppers

Directions:

1. Preheat oven to 350 degrees F (175 degrees C).
2. In a small bowl combine cheese and seasoning. After that, roll chicken pieces in cheese mixture to coat lightly. Set remaining cheese mixture aside.
3. Then, arrange coated chicken pieces in an 8x8x2 inch baking dish.
4. In a small saucepan, saute green onion in butter/margarine until tender.
5. Next, stir in flour, then add milk all at once. Simmer, stirring, until bubbly.
6. Stir in drained spinach and pimiento and combine together.
7. Spoon spinach mixture over chicken and sprinkle with remaining cheese mixture.
8. After that, bake uncovered for 30 to 35 minutes or until tender and chicken juices run clear. Delicious!

2. LAZY TOMATO SALSA

Ingredients:

- 3 tomatoes, chopped
- 1/2 cup finely diced onion
- 5 serrano chiles, finely chopped
- 1/2 cup chopped fresh cilantro

- 1 teaspoon salt

Directions:

1. In a mixing bowl, stir together tomatoes, onion, chili peppers, salt, and lime juice.
2. Then, chill for one hour in the refrigerator before serving.

3. HEARTY PAN-FRIED ASPARAGUS

Ingredients:

- 1/4 cup butter
- 2 tablespoons olive oil
- 3 cloves garlic, minced
- 1 pound fresh asparagus spears, trimmed

- pepper to taste

Directions:

1. Melt butter in a skillet over medium-high heat.
2. Afterwards, stir in the olive oil, salt, and pepper.
3. Cook garlic in butter for a minute, but do not brown.
4. After that, add asparagus, and cook for 10 minutes, turning asparagus to ensure even cooking.

4. EGG AND CHEESE BOATS

Ingredients:

- 2 oval sandwich rolls
- 4 eggs
- 3 tablespoons whole milk
- 1 (4 ounce) can chopped green chile peppers
- 1 cup shredded sharp Cheddar cheese
- 1/2 cup shredded pepper Jack cheese
- 1/2 teaspoon smoked paprika
- pepper to taste

Directions:

1. Preheat oven to 350 degrees F (175 degrees C). Next, line a rimmed baking sheet with parchment paper. Make a V-shaped cut in each roll, leaving the ends intact.

2. After that, lift out V-shaped wedge. Hollow out rolls gently to make shallow bread bowls, being careful not to cut through the bottom or sides.

3. Then, place bread bowls on the prepared baking sheet. Whisk eggs in a bowl. Add milk; whisk until well blended.

4. Stir in green chile peppers, Cheddar cheese, pepper Jack cheese, salt.

5. Next, pour mixture slowly into the prepared rolls, spreading evenly with a spoon.

6. After that, bake in the preheated oven until egg mixture is completely set and cheese is lightly browned, about 30 minutes.

7. Cool for 3 minutes before serving.

5. FAST CHICKEN STUFFED BAKED AVOCADOS

Ingredients:

- 4 avocados, halved and pitted
- 2 cooked chicken breasts, shredded
- 4 ounces cream cheese, softened
- 1/4 cup chopped tomatoes

- 1 pinch cayenne pepper
- 1/2 cup shredded Parmesan cheese, or more to taste
- salt to taste

Directions:

1. Preheat oven to 400 degrees F (200 degrees C).
2. Afterwards, scoop out some of the flesh in the center of each avocado; place into mixing bowl.
3. Now, add chicken, cream cheese, tomatoes, salt, cayenne pepper; mix nicely to combine.
4. Scoop spoonfuls of chicken mixture into the wells of each avocado; top each with generous amount of Parmesan cheese.
5. After that, place avocado halves, face-up, in muffin cups to stabilize.
6. Bake avocados in preheated oven until cheese is melted, 8 to 10 minutes.

6. THE BEST DEVILED EGGS

Ingredients:

- 6 eggs
- 1/4 cup mayonnaise
- 2 tablespoons finely chopped onion
- 3 tablespoons sweet pickle relish
- 1 tablespoon prepared horseradish
- 1 tablespoon prepared mustard
- paprika, for garnish
- pepper to taste

Directions:

1. Place eggs in a medium saucepan and cover with cold water.
2. Then, bring water to a boil and immediately remove from heat. After that, cover and let eggs stand in hot water for 10 to 12 minutes.
3. Remove from hot water, cool, peel and cut lengthwise.
4. Afterwards, remove yolks from eggs.
5. In a medium bowl, mash the yolks and mix together with mayonnaise, onion, horseradish and mustard.

6. With a fork or pastry bag, fill the egg halves with the yolk mixture.
7. Garnish with paprika, salt and pepper.
8. Chill until serving.

7. FAST DEVILED EGGS

Ingredients:

- 6 eggs
- 1/2 teaspoon paprika
- 2 tablespoons mayonnaise
- 1/2 teaspoon mustard powder

Directions:

1. Place eggs in a pot of salted water.

2. Next, bring the water to a boil, and let eggs cook in boiling water until they are hard boiled, approximately 10 to 15 minutes.

3. Afterwards, drain eggs, and let cool.

4. Cut eggs in half, lengthwise.

5. Remove the egg yolks and mash them together in a small mixing bowl.

6. Combine in the paprika, mayonnaise, and dry mustard.

7. Spoon mixture into the egg whites; cool and serve.

8. MINI HAM AND CHEESE ROLLS

Ingredients:

- 2 tablespoons dried minced onion
- 1 tablespoon prepared mustard
- 2 tablespoons poppy seeds
- 1/2 cup margarine, melted
- 24 dinner rolls
- salt to taste
- 1/2 pound chopped ham
- 1/2 pound thinly sliced Swiss cheese

Instructions:

1. Preheat oven to 325 degrees F (165 degrees C).
2. In a mixing bowl, mix onion flakes, mustard, poppy seeds and margarine.
3. After that, split each dinner roll.
4. Make a sandwich of the ham and cheese and the dinner rolls.
5. Afterwards, arrange the sandwiches on a baking sheet.
6. Drizzle the poppy seed mixture over the sandwiches. Bake for 20 minutes, or until cheese has melted.
7. Serve these sandwiches warm.

9. CALIFORNIA CHICKEN

Ingredients:

- 4 skinless, boneless chicken breasts
- 1 teaspoon olive oil
- 1/2 teaspoon onion powder
- 1 pinch ground black pepper
- 2 avocados
- 2 ripe tomatoes, sliced
- 1 package Monterey Jack cheese
- salt

Instructions:

1. Preheat oven to 350 degrees F (175 degrees C).
2. Now, warm oil in skillet and add chicken and onion.
3. Cook 15 minutes or until chicken is browned and just about done.
4. Now, add salt and pepper to taste.
5. Place chicken on cookie sheet and top each breast with 1 to 2 slices of tomato and 2 to 3 slices of cheese.
6. Afterwards, place in oven for 10 to 15 minutes, until cheese melts.
7. Remove from oven, add 2 to 3 slices of avocado on top of each breast, and serve immediately.

10.   BABY SPINACH OMELET

Ingredients:

- 2 eggs
- 1 cup torn baby spinach leaves
- 1 1/2 tablespoons grated Parmesan cheese
- 1/4 teaspoon onion powder
- 1/8 teaspoon ground nutmeg
- pepper to taste

Directions:

1. In a bowl, beat the eggs, and stir in the baby spinach and Parmesan cheese.
2. Then, season with onion powder, nutmeg, salt.
3. In a small skillet coated with cooking spray over medium heat, cook the egg mixture about 3 minutes, until partially set.
4. Next, flip with a spatula, and continue cooking 2 to 3 minutes.
5. Reduce heat to low, and continue cooking 2 to 3 minutes, or to desired doneness.

11. FAST AVOCADO CORN SALSA

Ingredients:

- 1 (16 ounce) package frozen corn kernels
- 2 (2.25 ounce) cans sliced ripe olives
- 1 red bell pepper
- 1 small onion
- 5 cloves garlic
- 1/3 cup olive oil
- 1/4 cup lemon juice
- 1 teaspoon dried oregano
- 1/2 teaspoon salt
- 1/2 teaspoon ground black pepper
- 4 avocados

Directions:

1. In a large bowl, combine corn, olives, red bell pepper and onion.
2. Next, in a small bowl, combine garlic, olive oil, lemon juice, oregano, salt and pepper.
3. Then, pour into the corn mixture and toss to coat.
4. Cover and chill in the refrigerator 8 hours, or overnight.
5. Stir avocados into the mixture before serving.

12. COCONUT DIRTY CHAI LATTE

Ingredients:

- 1 cup brewed chai tea
- 1 cup warm coconut milk
- 1 teaspoon instant espresso powder
- 1/2 teaspoon ground cinnamon
- 1 teaspoon honey
- pepper to taste

Directions:

1. Mix chai tea, coconut milk, espresso powder, and cinnamon in a blender; blend until smooth.

2. Pour into 2 mugs; drizzle with honey and sprinkle with shredded coconut.

13. CREAMY CAULIFLOWER TORTILLAS

Ingredients:

- 1 head cauliflower, finely grated
- 2 eggs
- pepper to taste

Directions:

1. Preheat oven to 400 degrees F (200 degrees C). Line a baking sheet with parchment paper.
2. Place cauliflower in a microwave-safe bowl.
3. Microwave at maximum power until tender, about 4 minutes. Next, place on a kitchen towel and squeeze out all liquid; transfer to a bowl.
4. Whisk eggs, salt, and black pepper in a bowl. Add to the cauliflower in batches; stir well.
5. Shape cauliflower mixture into 3-inch tortillas on the prepared baking sheet. Bake in the preheated oven until set, about 20 minutes.
6. Let cool slightly.
7. Heat a skillet over medium heat. Cook tortillas until golden brown, about 1 minute.
8. Flip and cook for 1 minute more.

14.   PEANUT BUTTER COOKIES

Ingredients:

- 1 cup peanut butter
- 1/2 cup low-calorie natural sweetener (such as Swerve(R))
- 1 egg
- 1 teaspoon sugar-free vanilla extract

Directions:

1. Preheat oven to 350 degrees F (175 degrees C). Line a baking sheet with parchment paper.
2. Combine peanut butter, sweetener, egg, and vanilla extract in a bowl; blend well until a dough is formed. Roll dough into 1-inch balls.
3. Place on the prepared baking sheet and press down twice with a fork in a criss-cross pattern.
4. Afterwards, bake in the preheated oven until edges are golden, 12 to 15 minutes.
5. Cool on the baking sheet for 1 minute before removing to a wire rack to cool completely.

15.   CHEESE CRISPS

Ingredients:

- 1 cup shredded Cheddar cheese

Directions:

1. Preheat oven to 400 degrees F (200 degrees C).
2. Line 2 baking sheets with parchment paper.
3. Arrange Cheddar cheese in 24 small heaps on the prepared baking sheets.
4. After that, bake in the preheated oven until golden brown, about 7 minutes.
5. Cool for 5 to 10 minutes before removing from baking sheets.

16. FLUFFY PANCAKES

Ingredients:

- 1 cup almond flour
- 1/4 cup coconut flour
- 2 tablespoons low-calorie natural sweetener
- 1 teaspoon baking powder
- 6 eggs, at room temperature
- 1/4 cup heavy whipping cream
- 2 tablespoons butter, melted
- 1 teaspoon vanilla extract
- salt to taste

Directions:

1. Mix almond flour, coconut flour, sweetener, salt, baking powder, and cinnamon together in a bowl.
2. Whisk in eggs, heavy cream, butter, and vanilla extract slowly until batter is just blended.
3. Heat a lightly oiled griddle over medium-high heat.
4. Then, drop batter by large spoonful onto the griddle and cook until bubbles form and the edges are dry, 3 to 4 minutes.
5. Flip and cook until browned on the other side, 2 to 3 minutes.
6. Repeat with remaining batter.

17. CHOCOLATE-PEANUT BUTTER CUPS

Ingredients:

- 1 cup coconut oil
- 1/2 cup natural peanut butter
- 2 tablespoons heavy cream
- 1 tablespoon cocoa powder
- 1 teaspoon liquid stevia
- 1/4 teaspoon vanilla extract
- 1 ounce chopped roasted salted peanuts

Directions:

1. Melt coconut oil in a saucepan over low heat, 3 to 5 minutes.
2. Stir in peanut butter until smooth. Afterwards, whisk in heavy cream, cocoa powder, liquid stevia, vanilla extract, and salt.
3. Pour chocolate-peanut butter mixture into 12 silicone muffin molds.
4. Sprinkle peanuts evenly on top. Place molds on a baking sheet.
5. Freeze chocolate-peanut butter mixture until firm, at least 1 hour.

6. Unmold chocolate-peanut cups and transfer to a resealable plastic bag or airtight container.

18.   OMELET WITH AVOCADO

- Ingredients
- 2 eggs (large)
- 1 tablespoon coconut oil or butter
- 2 tablespoons of water
- ½ avocado
- 1 serving pepper jack or cheddar cheese
- 1 tablespoon salsa (for topping)

Directions:

1. Beating the Eggs Start off by cracking two eggs into a bowl and adding 2 tablespoons of water.

2. Add salt and pepper to taste and whisk the eggs with a fork or hand whisk until the whites and yolks are thoroughly blended together.

3. Making the Omelet

4. Get out a nonstick skillet and pour in a tablespoon of butter or coconut oil, depending on your preference.

5. Heat the skillet on medium-high and note that the oil or butter will get hot very quickly.

6. Once the butter has melted, pour in the egg mixture.

7. You'll see that the mixture should start to set immediately.

8. Grab your spatula and gently pull all of the sides of the mixture toward the center.

9. When the edges are set but the inside is still soft, you're ready to add your filling ingredients.

10. For this recipe, just add cheese.

19. SCRAMBLED EGGS WITH SALMON

Ingredients

- 4 eggs
- 1 tablespoon milk or heavy cream
- Salt and pepper to taste
- 1 tablespoon butter
- ¼ pound smoked salmon, sliced OR ½ pound sautéed salmon fillet cut into cubes
- Dill or chive to taste (optional)

Directions:

1. Starting the Eggs
2. In a small bowl, whisk together the eggs, milk or heavy cream, salt and pepper.
3. Meanwhile, melt the butter in a nonstick skillet on medium high heat.
4. When the butter is melted, add in the egg mixture and use a wooden spoon or spatula to push around the eggs.
5. Adding the Salmon
6. While the cooking eggs still have a wet texture, add in the salmon.
7. You can use canned, smoked or cooked salmon chunks according to your preference.
8. Stir the salmon into the eggs and continue scrambling them until they're cooked to your liking.

20.   STEAK AND EGGS

Ingredients

- 8 ounces of flank steak (avoid cuts of steaks with excess amounts of fat or trim if needed)
- 1 tablespoon olive oil or butter
- 2-4 eggs
- 1 ounce of shredded cheese (pepper-jack works well)
- 1 tablespoon salsa (for topping)

Directions:

1. Cooking the steak In a large nonstick skillet, heat butter until foaming and melted on high heat.
2. Season the steak with salt and pepper to your liking and place in the skillet.
3. Instead of putting butter in the pan, you can also coat the steak with cooking spray (just make sure to choose butter-based cooking sprays without additives).
4. Reduce the heat and cook the steak for about 15 minutes, turning as needed to brown both sides.
5. Alternatively, you can sear the steak on high heat and then transfer it to an oven preheated to 350 degrees Fahrenheit.

Cook it in the oven for about 5 minutes until desired doneness (use a meat thermometer).

6. Once the steak is cooked, put it
7. onto a cutting board to rest and wipe out the excess juices from the skillet.
8. Cooking the Eggs
9. Using the same skillet, cook the eggs in any way you'd like.
10. To cook them sunny side up, simply crack the eggs into a skillet heated to high heat for about 3 minutes.
11. Scrambled also pairs well with the steak.

21.   BELGIAN WAFFLES

Ingredients:

- 1 cup bake mix
- 1 Tbsp baking powder
- 3 packets sugar substitute
- 1 tsp salt
- ¼ cup heavy cream
- 3 eggs
- 1 tsp vanilla
- ½ cup ice water

Instructions:

1. Heat a waffle iron. Whisk together the bake mix, baking powder, sugar substitute and salt.
2. Add cream, eggs, vanilla extract and ice water.
3. Pour in a little more water if necessary, 1 tablespoon at a time, until batter spreads easily.
4. Place approximately 3 tablespoons batter in center of waffle iron.
5. Cook according to manufacturer's directions until crisp and dark golden brown.
6. Repeat with remaining batter.

22.   FLAXSEED PANCAKE

Ingredients:

- 1 pinch cinnamon
- 1 tsp vanilla
- 2 tsp baking powder
- 6 Tbsp ground flax seed
- 1 cup egg beaters

Instructions:

1. Pour egg beaters into a bowl.

2. Add the remaining ingredients into the bowl. Mix well.

3. Set aside for 1 minute then mix again.

4. Put a skillet over medium heat and spray with oil.

5. Divide pancake mixture into four batches. Cook each batch as you would a regular pancake.

23. WHOLE-WHEAT CURRANT SCONES

Ingredients:

- ¼ cup currants
- 1 cup whole-wheat flour
- 1 cup Atkins Cuisine All Purpose Baking Mix
- 2 Tbsp granular sugar substitute

- 4 tsp baking powder
- 2 tsp ground ginger
- ⅛ tsp ground nutmeg
- ⅛ tsp salt
- 5 Tbsp cold unsalted butter, cut into pieces
- 2 large eggs, lightly beaten
- ¾ cup heavy cream

Instructions:

1.Heat oven to 400°F. Soak currants for 15 minutes in a cup of warm water.

2.Pulse flour, baking mix, sugar substitute, baking powder, ginger, nutmeg, and salt in a food processor. Add butter; pulse until well combined. Add eggs and heavy cream; pulse for 2 minutes. Drain currants and add; pulse until just combined.

3.Drop ¼-cup mounds on an ungreased baking sheet; press gently to flatten slightly. Bake until lightly golden, about 10 minutes.

4.Serve warm or at room temperature.

24.   PEANUT-STRAWBERRY BREAKFAST BARS

Ingredients:

- Olive oil cooking spray
- 1¼ cups old-fashioned rolled oats
- 1¼ cups granular sugar substitute
- ½ cup all purpose baking mix
- ¼ cup whole-wheat flour
- ¼ tsp salt
- ½ cup (1 stick) unsalted butter, melted

- 3 large eggs, lightly beaten
- ¾ cup unsweetened natural peanut butter
- ½ cup no-sugar-added strawberry jam

Instructions:

1. Heat oven to 350°F. Mist a 7-by-11-inch baking dish with cooking spray.
2. Mix oats, sugar substitute, baking mix, flour, and salt in a medium bowl; stir in butter and eggs until well combined.
3. Spread out half the dough in the baking dish.
4. Spread peanut butter evenly over dough; spread preserves evenly over peanut butter.
5. Crumble remaining dough over preserves.
6. Bake for about 25 minutes.
7. Cool completely before cutting into 12 pieces.

25. CRUNCHY TROPICAL BERRY AND ALMOND BREAKFAST PARFAIT

Ingredients:

- ½ cup heavy cream
- 1½ tsp granular sugar substitute, divided
- ¼ tsp coconut extract or pure vanilla extract
- ½ cup plain unsweetened whole-milk Greek yogurt
- 1 cup raspberries
- 1 cup blueberries or sliced strawberries
- 8 Tbsp Sweet and Salty Almonds
- ½ cup unsweetened shredded coconut, toasted

Instructions:

1. Combine cream, ½ tsp sugar substitute, and coconut extract or vanilla extract in a medium bowl; whip with an electric mixer for 3 minutes.
2. Add in the yogurt.
3. Mix raspberries and remaining sugar substitute in a blender until smooth.

4. In 4 parfait glasses, alternate layers of whipped cream, raspberry purée, blueberries, nuts, and shredded coconut, making two layers of each.

5. Serve right away.

26. CAULIFLOWER RICE SCRAMBLES

Ingredients:

- 1 head cauliflower, cut into florets (about 5 cups)
- 8 slices bacon
- 2 jalapeños, seeded and diced
- 8 large eggs

- 1 cup shredded cheddar cheese
- Hot sauce, to taste

Instructions:

1. Chop the cauliflower florets roughly in a food processor.
2. Warm the bacon in a large skillet over medium heat, and cook 4 to 5 minutes, stirring occasionally.
3. Transfer to a plate.
4. Do not discard the bacon grease.
5. Add the cauliflower and jalapeños to the bacon grease in the skillet, and cook 5 to 6 minutes, stirring often, until the cauliflower is soft.
6. Place the eggs and cheddar in a large bowl, and gently whisk. Add the eggs to the skillet and cook 3 to 4 minutes, stirring occasionally, until firm. Serve immediately with the bacon and hot sauce, if desired.

27.   BROILER HUEVOS RANCHEROS

Ingredients:

- Olive oil spray
- 2 chorizo sausage links, (about 6 ounces) thinly sliced
- 1 bunch asparagus, trimmed and chopped
- 2 cups broccoli florets
- 2 cups cauliflower florets
- 8 large eggs
- ½ cup commercial tomato salsa
- 1 ripe Hass avocado, cut into wedges
- ¼ cup sour cream

Instructions:

1. Set the oven to broil and coat a large skillet with olive oil spray.
2. Place over medium heat and add the chorizo, browning for 3 to 4 minutes, stirring well, until it renders its fat.
3. Add the asparagus, broccoli, and cauliflower, and cook 3 to 4 minutes, until the vegetables start to soften.
4. Crack the eggs on top.
5. Cook under the broiler on the middle oven rack for 3 to 4 minutes.
6. Serve immediately with the salsa, avocado, and sour cream.

28.   CHEESE PANCAKE

Ingredients:

- 1 Tbsp ground flax seed
- ½ tsp ground cinnamon
- 1 packet Stevia
- 4 oz cream cheese
- 2 eggs

Instructions:

1. Whisk the egg whites in a bowl.
2. In a separate bowl, beat the cream cheese with an electric mixer until smooth.
3. Combine the egg yolk with the cream cheese.
4. Add the flax seed, salt, stevia and cinnamon.
5. Continue to beat the mixture.
6. Fold in the beaten egg whites.
7. Put a pan over medium heat and add a small amount of butter.
8. Scoop ¼ cup from the mixture.
9. Cook the pancake for 3 minutes or until golden brown.
10. Then, serve.

29. CRANBERRY-ORANGE LOAF

Ingredients:

- 1 cup fresh or frozen cranberries, thawed
- 1¼ cups Atkins Bake Mix
- ½ cup walnuts, toasted and ground
- 16 packets sugar substitute

- 1 tsp baking soda
- ½ tsp salt
- 1 stick (8 Tbsp) butter, softened
- 2 Tbsp sour cream
- 2 eggs
- 1 Tbsp grated fresh orange zest
- 1 tsp vanilla extract
- 2 egg whites

Instructions:

1. Heat oven to 350°F Grease a 9-inch-by-5-inch loaf pan; set aside.
2. Coarsely chop cranberries; set aside. In a medium bowl, mix walnuts, sugar substitute, bake mix, baking soda and salt until combined.
3. In another bowl, beat butter 3 minutes with an electric mixer on medium, until fluffy.
4. Beat in sour cream, eggs, orange zest and vanilla extract. Fold in cranberries.
5. Combine together the bake mix mixture and butter mixture. In another bowl,
6. beat egg whites for about 2 minutes. In three portions, fold egg whites into batter.
7. Spoon batter into prepared pan. Bake 50 to 55 minutes.
8. Cool on wire rack.
9. Cut loaf into thin slices.

30. PANCAKES WITH RICOTTA-APRICOT FILLING

Ingredients:

- 3 eggs
- 3 Tbsp Atkins Bake Mix
- ¼ tsp salt
- ⅓ cup heavy cream;
- ¾ cup ricotta cheese
- ¼ cup sugar-free apricot jam
- 1 packet sugar substitute
- 1½ Tbsp butter

Instructions:

1. In a bowl, whisk eggs, bake mix and salt until smooth.
2. Gradually whisk in cream.
3. Set aside for 5 minutes.
4. Press ricotta through a fine sieve into a bowl.
5. Mix in jam and sugar substitute.
6. Melt butter in a nonstick skillet over medium heat.
7. Pour in 2 tablespoons batter and tilt skillet to coat bottom.
8. Cook until golden on bottom; turn over.
9. Cook 1 minute more.
10. Transfer to a plate.

11. Repeat with remaining batter. Spread pancakes with ricotta mixture, roll up and serve

31. ATKINS YORKSHIRE PUDDING

Ingredients:

- ½ cup Atkins Bake Mix
- ¼ cup wheat gluten
- 3 eggs
- 1 cup whole milk
- 1 tsp salt
- ⅓ cup beef drippings or vegetable oil

Instructions:

1. Heat oven to 450°F. Whisk together bake mix, gluten, eggs, milk and salt.
2. Pour drippings or oil into a muffin tin (½ tbsp each); place on centre rack in oven for 10 minutes, until smoky hot.
3. Add batter; bake 15 minutes.
4. Lower temperature to 350°F; cook 20 minutes more, until lightly browned.
5. Serve warm.

32. BIRDIES IN A BASKET

Ingredients:

- 1 Tbsp olive oil
- ½ bunch asparagus, trimmed and sliced
- ½ tsp seasoning salt
- 2 large green bell peppers, halved crosswise, seeded
- 4 large eggs
- 2 cups shredded cheddar cheese

Instructions:

1. Heat a skillet, and add the olive oil.
2. Add the asparagus and seasoning salt; cook 3 to 4 minutes, until the asparagus softens.
3. Transfer to a plate.
4. Preheat the oven to 350°F. Place the peppers in the skillet, stem side down, and sear for 1 minute over medium heat.
5. Flip and crack an egg into each pepper half.
6. Top with the asparagus and sprinkle with the cheddar.
7. Bake for 30 minutes, the whites of the eggs are cooked through.
8. Serve immediately.

33. GREEN EGGS AND HAM

Ingredients:

- 2 eggs
- 1/4 - 1/2 avacado
- salt and pepper slices of ham (or bacon)

Directions:

1. Hard boil the eggs and mash or chop them up while still warm.
2. Mix with the avocado to make a green egg salad.
3. Add salt and pepper to taste.
4. Lightly fry the slices of ham and serve with the egg salad.

5. I like to use the egg salad chilled and roll it up in slices of cold ham like a crepe.

34. SWISS CANADIAN BACON AND EGGS

Ingredients:

- 8 large eggs
- 1/4 cup milk
- 1/2 tea. Salt
- 1/4 tea. Pepper
- 1/3 cups finely chopped green onion, divided
- 4 oz swiss cheese

Directions:

1. Preheat broiler in medium mixing bowl whisk together eggs, milk, salt and pepper until well blended.
2. Stir in all but 2 tbl onions place 12" skillet over med-low heat until hot.
3. Coat skillet with cooking spray, add egg mixture.
4. Cover tightly; cook 14 min or until almost set arrange bacon in pinwheel on top of egg mixture.
5. Top with cheese; place under broiler 2 min or until cheese is bubbly; top with remaining 2tbls onion.
6. Cut into 4 wedges serve immediately

35.   PANCAKES OR WAFFLES

Ingredients:

- 1/2 cup Atkins Bake Mix;
- 1/4 cup FlaxSeed Meal (I used Bob's Red Mill w 0 net carbs);
- 1/4 cp Splenda (their website says the body does not recognize it as carbs);
- 1 egg- beaten;
- 3/4 cup water;
- 1/4 cup canola oil;1/2 tsp soda;
- 1 tsp baking powder;
- 1/4 cup heavy whipping cream (optional- if used add 4 GR);
- 1 tsp vanilla extract;
- 1 tsp maple flavoring.

Directions:

1. Heat griddle with oil or waffle iron.
2. Whisk together all ingredients in a medium bowl adding the water small amounts at a time until you get the consistency needed.

3. Spoon onto griddle or waffle iron.

4. Cook until crisp.

5. Serve with butter, cinnamon and/or low-carb syrup but remember to add any additional carbs from the syrup.

36. CRUSTLESS QUICHE LORRAINE

Ingredients:

- 5 eggs -- beaten
- 1 1/2 cups half & half or heavy cream
- 5 green onion -- snipped with scissors or small chopped onion

- ¼ green pepper chopped
- 1/2 cup spinach frozen or fresh
- 1/4 teaspoon salt
- 1/8 teaspoon pepper
- 3/4 cup bacon fried & crumbled
- 1 1/2 cups cheese (Cheddar, or Monterey, Swiss)

Directions:

Preheat oven to 350*

1. In lg. bowl beat eggs, add cream, mix.
2. Add all other ingredients and mix well. Pour egg mixture into a greased 9" or 10 " pie plate.
3. Place pie plate into a large baking dish and pour HOT water into the dish around the pie plate to a depth of 1 inch.
4. Bake quiche in the oven for 50 min. or until a knife inserted near center comes out clean.
5. Remove from oven.
6. Let stand for ten min.

37. CONFETTI SCRAMBLED EGGS

Ingredients:

- 3 eggs
- 1 Tbsp butter or olive oil
- 2 Tbsp chopped onion
- 2 Tbsp green bell pepper
- 1 Tbsp red bell pepper
- 2 ounce cheddar cheese
- 2 Tbsp chopped tomato (or salsa)
- 1 Tablespoon bacon bits

Directions:

1. In a small pan, melt butter (or add olive oil), add onion and bell pepper.
2. Cook till veggies are tender, add eggs.
3. Scramble till eggs are partially set, add the cheese.
4. Once done, remove from pan.
5. Sprinkle the tomato and bacon bits over the top.

38. EGG-IN-A-POT

Ingredients:

- 1 whole egg
- heavy cream
- 0.5 oz ham, sliced in small strips
- 0.5 oz grated cheddar
- any (fresh) herbs to taste
- salt
- pepper1tsp olive oil

Directions:

1. Grease an ovenproof ramekin with the olive oil.
2. Carefully break the egg into the ramekin, taking care not to break the yoke.
3. Add the ham and cheese and any herbs if you want.
4. Top up with the heavy cream to about a third of an inch below the rim of the ramekin.
5. Bake in a preheated oven of 350 degrees for about 20-25 minutes.

39.   SAUSAGE GRAVY

Ingredients:

- One roll of any breakfast sausage
- Approx 1/4 cup of water
- 1/2 teaspoon guar gum if necessary
- One pint of heavy whipping cream
- 1 egg

- salt and pepper to taste

Directions:

1. In a large skillet fry sausage until done.
2. Do not remove any of the grease from frying.
3. Turn down to low heat.
4. In a separate bowl whisk heavy cream and one egg together.
5. Add to the pan of sausage.
6. Salt and pepper to taste. You may need to add a small amount of water if it becomes too thick. Serve over low carb biscuits or eggs.
7. Entire recipe should be about 6-7 carbs or less and is wonderful.

40.   BLT RANCH OMELET

Ingredients:

- 2 each large eggs
- 1 tablespoon water
- 2 tablespoons shredded cheddar cheese
- 3 slices bacon -- cooked crisp and crumbled
- 1/2 small tomato -- sliced thin
- 1/2 cup shredded lettuce
- 1 tablespoon mayonnaise
- 1 tablespoon salsa

Directions:

1. Beat eggs with a fork and add water, beat again to mix.
2. Add salt and pepper if desired and beat into egg.
3. Heat bacon drippings and pour egg mixture into small, non-stick pan.
4. Cook over low heat until set and no longer wet looking.
5. Pile bacon, cheese, lettuce and tomato on one half and flip the other half over to cover.
6. Remove from heat and cover pan for 30 seconds to melt cheese.
7. Mix salsa and mayo and spread over omelette.

41.   BREAKFAST BLT ROLL-UPS

Ingredients:

- 4 each romaine lettuce leaves

- 1 tablespoon mayonnaise

- 3 slices bacon -- cooked crisp and crumbled

- 4 tablespoons shredded cheddar cheese

- 1/2 small roma tomato -- diced

Directions:

1. Shred 2 of the romaine leaves.
2. Mix shredded lettuce, mayo, cheese, bacon and tomato.
3. Add a little salt and pepper to taste.
4. Fill remaining 2 romaine leaves w/mixture, fold and enjoy.

42.   WONDER WAFFLES

Ingredients:

- 2 Tbls. heavy cream
- 2 Tbls. water (0 carbs)
- 1 Tsp. vanilla extract
- 2 Pkt. Splenda (or 2 tsp. powdered Splenda)
- 2 or 3 ounces of crushed pork rinds
- 1/4 Tsp. ground cinnamon
- 3 Tbls. melted butter

Directions:

1. Beat the eggs then add the cream, water, and vanilla extract and beat some more.
2. Mix the Splenda with the cinnamon and then add that to the eggs.
3. When well blended mix in the ground pork rinds.
4. Let the mixture sit for a couple of minutes until it thickens. Then stir and check the consistency.
5. It should be quite thick, but not to thick to spoon easily. If too thick, add a little water.
6. If too thin, add a little bit more pork rinds.

7. Just before you're ready to put into waffle iron, stir in about 2/3 of the melted butter.

43.   MOCK DANISH

Ingredients:

- 3 oz cream cheese
- 1 egg, beaten
- 1/4 tsp vanilla extract
- dash of cinnamon
- 1 packet Splenda

Directions:

1. Heat the cream cheese in a small saucepan at low-medium heat till it is melted and creamy, stirring constantly.

2. Then, add the beaten egg, and begin whisking the mixture to really mix it well.
3. It will thicken as it cooks.
4. Continue whisking it, to keep it smooth.
5. When it starts to thicken, add the sweetener and seasonings.
6. Let it cook until it is very thick, thicker than pudding.
7. When it holds its shape on a spoon, it's done.
8. Chill and eat.

44. MEDITERRANEAN FRITTATA

Ingredients:

- 8 pitted kalamata olives (black olives will do in a pinch)
- 1 med. zucchini, cut into 1/2" cubes (about 2 cups)
- 1 sweet red pepper, diced
- 1/2 cup chopped onion
- 1/4 cup olive oil9 large eggs, lightly beaten
- 1/2 (4 ounce) package crumbled feta cheese
- 1/3 cup thinly sliced fresh basil
- 1/2 tsp salt
- 1/2 tsp freshly ground pepper
- 1/3 cup freshly grated Parmesan cheese
- basil sprigs for garnish

Directions:

1. Cook first 4 ingredients in hot oil in a 10" ovenproof skillet over med-high heat, stirring constantly, until vegetables are tender.
2. Combine eggs and next 4 ingredients; pour into skillet over vegetables.
3. Cover and cook over med-low heat 10 to 12 minutes or until almost set.
4. Remove from heat, and sprinkle with Parmesan cheese.

5. Broil 5 1/2" from heat (with electric oven door partially opened) 2 to 3 minutes or until golden.
6. Cut frittata into wedges; garnish, if desired.
7. Serve warm or at room temperature.

45. BREAKFAST EGG CASSEROLE

Ingredients:

- 6-12 eggs
- 1/2 cup crumpled bacon
- salt and pepper to taste
- garlic powder to taste1/4 cup onion
- 1/4 cup hot peppers (option)

- 1/2 cup broccoli (option)
- 2 tbsp heavy cream

Directions:

1. In a 9x13 pan mix all with a whisk.
2. Bake at 350 for 20-30 mins depending on how many eggs.
3. When done set slices of cheese to melt.
4. When cool, slice into 9 slice and freeze the rest for another day

46. SWEET INDUCTION
BREAKFAST

Ingredients:

- 1/2 tablespoon butter
- 2 eggs
- 2 packets artificial sweetener2 tablespoons cream cheese
- 1 teaspoon heavy cream
- 1/2 teaspoon vanilla

Directions:

1. Heat frying pan and allow butter to coat the bottom.
2. Mix the 2 eggs with a packet of sweetener in a small bowl and pour into frying pan.
3. In another small bowl mix the cream cheese, heavy cream, vanilla and a packet of sweetener.
4. When the eggs are cooked, you can let them cool before adding the cream mixture or let the mixture melt slightly onto the warm eggs.
5. Gently spread the cream mixture to cover the eggs (like tomato sauce on a pizza).
6. Using a spatula roll the egg "crepe" together like a jelly roll.

47.   PORRIDGE

Ingredients:

- 1 egg
- 2 teaspoons protein powder -- soy, unflavoured half and half
- 1/4 cup powdered nuts (macadamia -- walnut, whatever)
- Sweetener

Directions:

1. As a note, just put the nuts into a blender and let it run enough to chop them into a coarse powder.
2. Mix the protein powder and the egg in a small mixing bowl. Add an equivalent volume of half and half, or cream.
3. Mix. Put the bowl in the microwave and cook on high for 1 1/2 minutes.
4. Mix again, and cook for 1 minute.
5. Adjust the time so that the mixture is cooked and not runny.
6. Mix again until it has the consistency of porridge. Mix in the nuts.
7. Add sweetener to taste, and add half and half as typical on porridge.
8. The result is pretty adequate with a slight eggy taste.

48. BANANA NUT PORRIDGE

Ingredients:

- 2 Eggs
- 2 tablespoons water
- 2 tablespoons heavy cream
- 2 teaspoons sweetener
- 1 tablespoon psyllium
- husks1 tablespoon butter
- 1/2 cap vanilla flavoring
- 1/2 cap banana flavoring
- 1 good shake cinnamon
- 1 light shake nutmeg

Directions:

1. Beat all the ingredients, leaving 1 tbl cream and 1 tsp sweetener as topping.
2. Melt the butter in a skillet over medium heat, pour in the egg mixture.
3. Fold about 3 or 4 times. When the eggs just set, remove from heat & then put into bowl.
4. Sprinkle the remaining sweetener & add cream over the top.
5. In OWL a tbl of chopped Walnuts is nice.

49. SWEET CINNAMON PANCAKE

Ingredients:

- 2 eggs
- 1 ounce cream cheese
- 2 splenda packets -- (2 to 3)1 teaspoon heavy cream
- 1 teaspoon cinnamon -- (1 to 2)
- butter

Directions:

1. Melt cream cheese in microwave.
2. Mix in eggs, splenda, cream and cinnamon.
3. Melt butter on a frying pan and pour mixture

50. FRENCH TOAST RECIPE

Ingredients:

- Two whole eggs
- tsp cinnamon
- 1 tbsp of Splenda granular or 1 packet of Splenda

Directions:

1. Combine ingredients.
2. Preheat skillet over medium heat and add 2 tbsp of Life Services High Oleic Sunflower Oil.
3. Beat mixture thoroughly with a fork and dip sliced Keto Cinnamon Bread in batter and fry until golden brown.
4. Enjoy with Keto Syrup and/or Betta Butta.

51. BREAKFAST BREAD

Ingredients:

- 1/4 cup protein powder
- 1/2 cup carbo-lite bake mix
- 1/4 cup flax seeds – ground into 1/2C meal
- 3 large eggs
- 1/2 cup sour cream1/4 cup water
- 1/2 teaspoon salt
- 2 teaspoons baking powder
- 3 tablespoons melted
- butter

Directions:

1. Preheat oven to 350f. Spray a standard 8" loaf pan (or an 8x8x2 cake pan) with cooking spray.
2. Mix dry ingredients in a large bowl.
3. Beat eggs with a fork and blend in butter, water and sour cream. Stir into dry ingredients until just blended.
4. Pour into prepared pan and bake: 30 minutes for square pan and 40 minutes for loaf pan.
5. This bread is semi-sweet because the carbo-lite bake mix has splenda in it.

52.　TURKEY CLUB OMELETTE

Ingredients:

- 3 Eggs
- 1/4 cup cubed turkey breast meat
- 2 strips bacon – cooked and chopped
- 2 tablespoons sour cream2 sprigs chives – coarsely chopped
- 2 slices tomato slices -- chopped
- 1/4 cup hollandaise sauce

Directions:

1. Prep all of your ingredients ahead of time.
2. Cook the eggs on one side and flip to other side.
3. Add ingredients and fold or roll.
4. Add hollandaise sauce over the top of omelette.

53.   WAGON WHEEL FRITTATA

Ingredients:

- 1 tablespoon cooking oil
- 10 ounces frozen broccoli spears
- 1 tablespoon water
- 4 ounces button mushrooms -- drained
- 6 eggs2 tablespoons heavy cream
- 3 tablespoons water
- 1 1/2 teaspoons Italian seasoning -- crushed
- 6 thin tomato slices -- about
- 1 med tomato
- 1/4 cup grated Parmesan cheese

Directions:

1. In a 10-inch omelet pan or skillet over medium heat, combine oil, broccoli, and water.
2. Cover and cook just until broccoli can be broken apart with a fork, about 3 minutes.
3. Take pan off the heat.
4. Arrange broccoli spears so stems point to center of pan.
5. Set mushrooms, rounded sides up, between broccoli spears.

6. In medium bowl, thoroughly blend eggs, milk, and seasoning.
7. Pour over broccoli.
8. Cover and cook over medium heat until eggs are almost set.
9. Remove from heat.

TURKEY AND HAM FRITTATA

Ingredients:

- 1 cup chopped cooked turkey
- 1 cup chopped ham
- 6 eggs
- 3 tablespoons oil
- 2 medium tomatoes --
- chopped1 cup button mushroom -- diced
- 4 shallots -- chopped
- 1/2 cup heavy cream
- salt and ground black pepper for seasoning

Directions:

1. Put oil in large frying pan, add turkey, ham and mushrooms until mushrooms are tender.
2. Add tomatoes and onions.
3. Cook, stirring for 2 minutes.
4. In a bowl whisk together eggs, cream and seasoning, then pour into turkey and ham mixture in pan.
5. Cook gently until mixture is firm - the top will not be quite set.
6. Place pan under a hot griller to complete cooking the top for approx. 2 minutes.
7. Turn frittata on board and cut into wedges.
8. This recipe is great when you have all that leftover turkey and ham.

55. **Butterflied Leg of Lamb**

Ingredients:

- 1 ½ servings Atkins Cuisine Bread
- 3 ½ lbs. leg of lamb (butterflied)
- 1 tsp. fresh rosemary (chopped)
- 1 tsp. salt
- ½ tsp. pepper
- ¼ cup Dijon mustard
- 1/3 cup fresh parsley (chopped)
- 2 cloves of garlic (minced)

Directions:

1. Preheat oven to 200°F and place bread inside. Remove after 15 minutes, or until they become dry but not browned. Raise oven temperature to 375°F.

2. While oven is heating, put the bread in a food processor and pulse until they turn into fine crumbs. Put it in a bowl and combine with garlic and parsley. Set aside.

3. Rub the lamb legs with rosemary, salt and pepper then place them on a roasting pan. Spread mustard over them. Pat each leg gently with the bread crumb mixture.

4. Cook lamb in the oven for around 45 minutes or, if you have a meat thermometer, until internal temperature reaches 135°F. (This is for medium-rare. You may adjust this to suit your preferred doneness).

5. Let it rest for 15 minutes before carving. Serve.

56.   Baked Chicken with Broccoli

Ingredients

For the chicken:

- 2 chicken breasts, skinless and boneless
- 2 tablespoons olive oil
- Salt and pepper to taste

For the broccoli:

- 1 head broccoli, cut into florets
- 2 tablespoons olive oil
- 1 teaspoon lemon juice
- 1 clove of garlic

- Salt and pepper to taste

Directions:

1. Preparing the Ingredients. Preheat the oven to 400 degrees Fahrenheit.
2. You can choose to cook the chicken and broccoli on one pan, or cook the chicken separately on a broiler pan and the broccoli on a baking sheet.
3. Slice the chicken breasts in half down the sides so you get four thinner slices of chicken breast halves.
4. Season with salt and pepper and rub them with olive oil on both sides.
5. Making sure to wash your hands after touching the chicken, take the broccoli florets and toss them in a bowl with olive oil, salt, pepper, lemon juice and garlic.
6. Spread the chicken and broccoli on a baking sheet in an even layer.
7. The chicken should take about 10 minutes to bake on the first side; after that, flip the chicken into individual portion sizes to eat throughout the week.
8. Cooked chicken lasts in the fridge for 3 to 4 days, so freeze portions as needed. Instead of broccoli, try the chicken with Brussel sprouts or asparagus and cook for another 15 minutes.
9. Use a meat thermometer to tell when the chicken is done (it should read 165 degrees Fahrenheit).

10. The broccoli will take about 15 to 20 minutes, depending on how tender you like them.
11. Once you've removed the chicken and broccoli from the oven, allow to cool and distribute into individual portions (about 4 ounces of chicken with a half a cup of broccoli).
12. Squirt a little bit of lemon juice on top for extra flavor.
13. In later phases of the Atkins diet, pair the chicken with brown rice or quinoa.

57. Salad with Hard Boiled Egg

Ingredients

- 2 eggs
- 2 cups lettuce
- ½ cucumber, sliced
- 1 handful radishes, sliced
- 1 stalk celery, cut into pieces
- 1 tablespoon full-fat dressing (without sugar)
- 1 teaspoon lemon juice

Directions:

1. Boiling the Eggs. The easiest way to boil eggs is to put them in a pot and cover them with cold water, making sure to put in the eggs first so they don't crack. Bring the pot to a rolling boil on high heat.

2. As soon as you have a rolling boil, take the pot off the burner and cover with a lid.

3. This is when the eggs are actually cooked.

4. The eggs should sit in the hot water, covered, for about 15 to 17 minutes, with larger eggs needing more time.

5. Once cooked, drain the water from the eggs and let them sit in a bowl of ice water to cool them down – do this for an hour or so if you want to have an easier time peeling them.

6. Making the Salad Using a cutting board and a sharp knife, carefully chop all of the vegetables into bite sized pieces according to your preference.

7. Mix the vegetables together and toss in your choice of dressing and the lemon juice. Make sure the dressing you use is sugar free.

8. Serve two cups of the salad into a bowl and top with one or two boiled eggs or your choice of protein.

9. If you're not feeling like eggs, try the salad with avocado or boiled chicken as a topping instead.

58. Chicken Broth

Ingredients

- 1 whole chicken, fat and giblets removed
- 2 celery stocks
- 6-8 baby carrots or 3-4 medium carrots
- 1 onion
- 2-3 garlic cloves
- 1 teaspoon peppercorns
- 12-16 cups of water (as needed)
- Salt and pepper to taste

Directions:

1. Preparing the Ingredients. Cut the celery stocks in half. Peel and quarter the onion.
2. If you're using medium carrots, cut them in quarters. Gather everything together and get out a large cooking pot.
3. Place all the ingredients, chicken first, in the pot and fill with water until just covering the chicken with an inch or two above.
4. Heat the pot on medium high heat and bring to a boil. At this point, you'll want to reduce it to a simmer.
5. You may need to skim the fat from the surface using a spoon Allow the pot to simmer for one to 1 1/2 hours.

6. Make sure the chicken is cooked through.

7. Remove the chicken and cut away the meat.

8. Allow the chicken to cool and store the meat for salads, snacks and other meals.

9. Continuing simmering the broth and add in the bones and carcass from the chicken.

10. Simmer for an hour and remove from heat, allow to cool (it should get to room temperature before being stored).

11. Discard the bones and strain the broth.

12. Let cool and store in the fridge for 6-7 days of freeze for up to 3 months.

59. Chicken and Vegetable Stir-fry

Ingredients

- 2 boneless skinless chicken breasts
- 2 tablespoons peanut oil or olive oil
- 2 cups mixed frozen vegetables
- ½ small onion, minced
- 1-2 garlic cloves, minced

- 1 tablespoon of ginger, freshly minced
- 1 tablespoon low sodium soy sauce
- Salt and pepper to taste

Directions:

1. Cut the chicken breast into bite sized pieces and season with salt and pepper.
2. Heat ½ tablespoon of oil in over medium high heat and cook the chicken, stir frying for about 5 or 6 minutes until the chicken is cooked through.
3. Once cooked, set the chicken aside and save the pan for the vegetables.
4. Heat ½ tablespoon of oil over medium-high heat and add in the onions and garlic.
5. Once translucent and fragrant, add in the frozen vegetables and cook for 3 or 4 minutes until tender yet crispy on the edges.
6. Add back in the chicken and soy sauce to the vegetables and toss together.
7. For added flavor, allow the stir fry to simmer, but make sure that the sauce is well distributed.
8. Divide the stir fry into four separate servings and enjoy or store in the fridge for 3 to 4 days.

60. Balsamic Pork Loin with Roasted Cauliflower

Ingredients:

- 1 ¼ lbs. pork tenderloin
- 4 cups cauliflower florets
- 2 tbsp. extra virgin olive oil
- 1 tsp. dried rosemary
- ½ tsp. salt
- For marinade:
- ¼ cup olive oil
- ¼ cup balsamic vinegar
- 2 tsp. ground mustard seed
- 1 tsp. garlic powder
- 2 tsp. salt
- 1 tsp. ground black pepper.
- ¼ tsp. ground allspice

Directions:

1. Before making dish, marinate pork at least 2 hours ahead, or have it marinating in the fridge overnight for added flavor. Combine all the ingredients for the marinade in a re-sealable plastic bag. Place the pork inside the bag and shake well to distribute marinade evenly. Squeeze out the air and seal the bag.

Refrigerate.

2. Preheat the oven to 350°F. Empty contents of plastic bag, including marinade, into a glass baking dish. Bake pork for about an hour, basting it 3 to 4 times, until the meat's internal temperature reaches 145°F.

3. Meanwhile, toss cauliflower with the olive oil, rosemary and salt in a large bowl. Arrange cauliflower on a separate baking sheet and place it in the oven with the pork. Allow it to bake for 40 to 50 minutes, until they turn light brown and tender, then remove from oven.

4. Remove pork from oven and let it stand for 5 to 10 minutes. Slice into desired thickness and serve with the cauliflower.

61.   Broiled Lobster In Garlic Oil

Ingredients:

- ¼ cup extra virgin olive oil
- 2 cloves garlic (chopped finely)
- 1 tbsp. butter (unsalted, melted)
- 3 lbs. (6 pcs.) live lobsters
- 1/8 tsp. salt (preferably kosher salt)

Directions:

1.Assemble broiler rack around 6 inches away from the flame. Heat the broiler.

2.Mix together the olive oil, garlic and butter. Set aside and keep warm.

3.Meanwhile, place the lobsters on a cutting board. Hold them down firmly and, with a Chinese cleaver or a sharp chef's knife, split each one in half, from the head to its end.

4.Using a small hammer, meat mallet, or the spine of a knife, gently strike their claws to crack them.

5.From behind the mouth parts, scoop out their viscera and then remove the green roe sacs. Transfer lobsters onto the broiling pan with their cut side facing up.

6.Brush lobsters with a liberal amount of the butter mixture. Sprinkle with a small pinch of salt to taste.

7.Let them broil for 4 minutes then baste with the butter mixture.

8.Let them broil for 3 more minutes and serve while hot

62.   Coconut Garlic Spice Prawns

Ingredients

- 16 ounces raw prawns or shrimp (without shell, deveined)
- 4-6 garlic cloves, minced
- ½ teaspoon curry powder
- ½ teaspoon chili powder
- ½ teaspoon red pepper flakes
- 1 tablespoon coconut oil
- ¼ coconut milk
- 1 tablespoon fresh parsley or chopped green onions
- 1 teaspoon lemon juice

Directions:

1. Heat a large nonstick skillet on medium heat with 1 tablespoon coconut oil.
2. Add in the minced garlic and cook until fragrant, stirring frequently.
3. Clean the prawns and pat dry with a paper towel, then add the prawns into the skillet.
4. Season the prawns with chili powder, chili flakes and curry powder.
5. Cook the prawns until they turn pink.
6. Once the prawns turn pink, pour in the coconut milk.
7. Continue cooking until the milk begins to bubble.
8. Add salt and pepper as needed.
9. Remove the prawns from heat and serve warm with a little bit of fresh parsley or green onions and a squirt of fresh lime juice.
10. You can also add in cooked vegetables (just add them to the skillet with the shrimp until heated through).

63. Grilled Fish with Green Beans

Ingredients

- 2 tablespoons olive oil
- 2 fillets of halibut, cod or other white fish of your choice
- 1-2 tablespoons lemon juice
- 1 tablespoon chopped fresh parsley
- 1 teaspoon dried thyme leaves, chopped
- 1 garlic clove, minced
- 1 bag frozen or fresh green string beans
- 2 tablespoons butter
- Salt and pepper to taste

Directions:

1. Mix together 1 tablespoon of olive oil, the lemon juice, thyme and garlic together in a bag.
2. Season the fish with salt and pepper and put into the bag with the marinade.
3. Set the bag into the fridge and allow to marinate an hour. When you're ready to cook it, heat your grill to high and put a little bit of oil on the grate (if you're dealing with extra flaky fish, you may need to use a grill basket).
4. Cook the fish for about 4 minutes on both sides until cooked through.

5. The fish should flake easily with a fork.

6. In the meantime, put one tablespoon of olive oil in a skillet heated to medium-high. Add in the green beans. Using a fresh lemon, add at least 1 teaspoon of lemon zest.

7. Season as needed and cook for about five minutes. You want the green beans to be tender yet crisp.

8. Divide the fish fillet into serving sizes (about 6 ounces cooked), and serve with green beans.

9. Add butter on top of the fish and green beans for added richness and flavor.

10. Garnish with fresh parsley.

64. Stuffed Parmesan Mushrooms (Vegetarian)

Ingredients

- 1 tablespoon coconut oil or olive oil
- 4 large portabella mushrooms

- 2-3 sundried tomatoes, diced
- 2 cups baby spinach, cut into bite sized pieces
- 2-3 garlic cloves, minced
- ½ sweet onion, diced into pieces
- 1/3 cup grated Parmesan
- ¼ feta cheese or mozzarella
- Salt and pepper to taste

Steps

1. Clean the mushrooms thoroughly using a damp paper towel to wipe the entire mushroom.
2. Trim the stalks (you can eat the stem if you choose).
3. Use a spoon to remove the gills on the underside of the mushroom (you can also eat these if you want).
4. In a pan over medium high heat, add in the oil and sauté the onions.
5. After about 3 minutes, add in the tomatoes and cook for another minute or two.
6. As the onions the onions become translucent, add in the garlic, cook until fragrant, and then add in the baby spinach.
7. Once all the ingredients are tender and the spinach is melted, remove from heat.
8. Add seasonings and Parmesan into the mixture and generously and evenly stuff the mushrooms.

9. While you're working on the ingredients, preheat your oven to 375 degrees Fahrenheit.

10. Once you've stuffed your mushrooms, set the mushrooms onto a baking sheet and bake for about 30 minutes.

11. Open up the oven and put the feta or mozzarella cheese on top and continue cooking for another 10 minutes or until the mixture before baking.

12. Cheese is melted and slightly golden.

65.   Chilean Sea Bass In Curry Broth And Seared Ginger

Ingredients:

- 2 tbsp. canola oil
- 48 oz. sea bass fillets
- 1/3 cup ginger root (cut into thin matchsticks)
- 14 ½ oz. of chicken broth
- 1 medium-sized red bell pepper (cut into ¼-inch strips)
- 1 scallion (cut diagonally into thin slices)
- 1 tbsp. tomato paste

- ½ tsp. Thai red curry paste
- ¼ tsp. salt
- ½ cup cilantro (chopped finely)

Directions:

1. Heat oil in a skillet over medium heat.
2. Add the ginger and cook until brown, stirring constantly for 2 to 3 minutes.
3. Remove ginger with a slotted spoon, transfer to a small bowl or plate and set aside.
4. Discard oil. Pour broth into the skillet and put a vegetable steamer basket in it.
5. Arrange sliced bell peppers on the steamer and then place sea bass over them. Sprinkle with salt.
6. Leave uncovered and bring it to a boil over medium-high heat.
7. Once it boils, cover skillet and reduce to medium heat.
8. Check after 10 to 12 minutes and turn off heat if fish has turned opaque.
9. Remove the steamer basket form the skillet and remove fish and bell pepper using a slotted spoon.
10. Transfer to a plate and sprinkle with sliced scallion.
11. Cover plate loosely with a foil and set aside.
12. Whisk in the tomato paste in the broth in the skillet. Add the curry paste and reduce heat to low.

13. Let it simmer for 2 minutes then turn off heat. (If desired, you may add more curry paste to adjust level of spice.)
14. Place fish and bell pepper in serving bowls and pour around 2 tablespoons of broth around the fish fillets.
15. Sprinkle with a tablespoon of chopped cilantro and serve topped with a teaspoon of seared ginger.

66. Fillet Mignons With Bacon And Gorgonzola Butter

Ingredients:

- 12 oz. fillet mignons (2 fillets, around 6 oz. each)
- 2 strips bacon
- ¼ tsp. salt
- ¼ tsp/ freshly ground pepper
- 2 tsp. extra virgin olive oil
- 1 small scallion

- 2 tbsp. Gorgonzola cheese (crumbled)
- 2 tbsp. butter (unsalted, softened)
- ½ lb. mixed mushrooms (cremini, Portobello, shiitake, and/or oyster mushrooms; sliced)

Directions:

1. Pre-heat oven to 425°F and arrange rack in the center.

2. Meanwhile, sprinkle the fillets with 1/8 teaspoon each of salt and pepper.

Wrap the side of each fillet with a slice of bacon, using a toothpick to secure it into place.

3. Heat the oil in a large nonstick skillet over medium-high heat. Cook fillets for around 5 minutes or until browned, using a pair of tongs to turn them frequently to avoid scorching any side.

4. Transfer fillets to a rimmed baking sheet and roast it in the oven for 7 to 10 minutes for a rare fillet. If you wish to control its doneness, insert an instant read meat thermometer in the center of each fillet. (135°F – medium rare; 145°F – medium; 160°F – medium-well done; 180°F – well done)

5. While beef is roasting, prepare the Gorgonzola butter. Slice the white portion of the scallion thinly and set it aside. Take the green portion and chop finely. Place in a small bowl, add the cheese and butter, and combine. Set aside.

6. Using the same skillet where you cooked the fillets, cook the mushrooms and the white portion of the scallion over medium-high heat. Add the remaining salt and pepper. Lower heat and cook for about 4 minutes or until mushrooms turn tender, stirring frequently so they don't burn.

7. Put the mushrooms on two serving plates and top with the roasted fillets. Serve with Gorgonzola butter.

67. Mediterranean Spice-Crusted Lamb

Ingredients:

- 2 tsp. coriander (ground)
- 1 tsp. cinnamon (ground)
- 1 tsp. cumin powder
- 1 tsp. salt
- ½ tsp. black pepper (freshly ground)
- 4 lbs. leg of lamb (tied)
- 1 ½ cup pomegranate juice (optional)
- 1 cup arugula leaves (shredded)
- 1 tbsp. fresh chives (chopped)

Directions:

1. Heat oven to 450°F. Meanwhile, in a small bowl, combine the coriander, cinnamon, cumin, salt and pepper. Rub the mixture over lamb.

2. Place lamb in the oven and let it roast for 15 minutes. Lower the temperature to 350°F and let it cook for another 35 minutes or until an instant-read thermometer shows meat is 130°F.

3. Transfer lamb to a cutting board and cover with foil. Let it stand for 10 minutes.

4. If desired, bring pomegranate juice to a boil and let it cook until sauce is reduced by half. (Add 6.5g to Net Carb count if using) Scrape up any browned bits from the sauce and skim off the fat.

5. Garnish lamb with arugula and chives. Serve with pomegranate sauce.

68.   Pork Ribs in Chili Maple-Mustard Syrup

Ingredients:

- 4 lbs. pork ribs
- ½ tsp. salt
- 1.2 tsp. pepper
- 1 tbsp. canola oil
- 1 small onion (chopped coarsely)
- 4 oz. maple syrup (must be sugar-free)
- 3 tbsp. Dijon mustard

- 3 tbsp. red wine vinegar
- 1 tbsp. chili powder

Directions:

1. Pre-heat oven (or grill) to 325°F. Sprinkle the ribs with salt and pepper and set aside.

2. To prepare glaze, heat oil in a medium saucepan set over medium heat for about a minute. Sauté onions for 4 minutes, until they turn soft. Add the maple syrup, mustard, vinegar and chili powder. Lower heat and let it simmer for 15 to 20 minutes until it slightly thickens.

3. Place ribs on a baking sheet (or grill) and cover with foil. Bake it for 45 minutes then remove foil, brush with glaze and bake for another 45 minutes, occasionally turning and brushing with glaze. Serve.

69. Mushroom-Herb-Stuffed Chicken Breasts

Ingredients:

- 3 Tbsp butter, divided
- ½ pound fresh shiitake mushrooms, wiped clean, trimmed, and minced
- ½ small yellow or white onion, minced
- 2 cloves garlic, minced
- 2 Tbsp dry sherry
- 3 Tbsp chopped fresh parsley
- ½ tsp chopped fresh thyme
- ¾ tsp salt, divided
- ⅛ tsp freshly ground black pepper
- 4 bone-in chicken breast halves (about 2 pounds) with skin

Instructions:

1. Heat oven to 400°F.

2. Melt 2 Tbsp butter in a skillet. Add mushrooms and onion; sauté until mushrooms have released their liquid, about 5

minutes. Stir in garlic and sherry; cook 1 minute longer. Remove from heat; stir in parsley, thyme, ½ tsp salt, and pepper.

3.Using a thin sharp knife, cut a pocket in the thicker part of each breast, stuff mushroom mixture into pockets.

4.Set chicken, skin side up, in a 9-by-13-inch baking pan. Melt remaining tablespoon butter and brush on chicken. Season with remaining ¼ teaspoon salt. Bake until cooked through, about 35 minutes. Serve warm.

70.   Jerk Chicken

Ingredients:

- 6 scallions, sliced
- 2 cloves garlic, minced
- 3 Scotch bonnet chili peppers, seeded and minced
- ¼ cup canola oil
- 2 Tbsp freshly squeezed lime juice
- 2 Tbsp ground allspice
- 4 tsp mustard powder
- 2 tsp salt
- 2 tsp granular sugar substitute
- 1 tsp ground cinnamon

- 4 bone-in, skin-on chicken breast halves

Instructions:

1.Combine all ingredients except the chicken in a food processor or blender; purée. Transfer to a resealable plastic bag or glass baking dish; add chicken and turn to coat. Refrigerate overnight, turning once.

2.Heat oven to 450°F.

3.Line a baking sheet with foil. Remove chicken from marinade, letting excess drain off; transfer to the baking sheet. Bake until just cooked through, 30–40 minutes. Serve.

71.   Roast Beef with Greek Yogurt-Horseradish Sauce

Ingredients:

- 1 tsp garlic salt
- 1 tsp sweet paprika
- 1 tsp freshly ground black pepper
- 1 (5-pound) top or bottom round beef roast

Horseradish Sauce

- 2 Tbsp grated fresh horseradish
- 1 cup full-fat Greek yogurt
- 1 Tbsp lemon juice
- 1 cucumber, peeled, seeded, and grated

Instructions:

1.Preheat the oven to 375°F.

2.To make the sauce, place the horseradish, yogurt, lemon juice, and cucumber in a medium bowl. Stir well to combine, and refrigerate.

3.Place the garlic salt, paprika, and pepper in a small bowl, and mix well with a spoon. Sprinkle the roast with the spices, and transfer to a 2-quart baking dish.

4.Transfer the roast to the oven, and cook for 1 hour to 1 hour 30 minutes. Set aside for 5 minutes to allow the juices to redistribute.

5.Slice the roast beef, and serve immediately with the Horseradish Sauce.

72.   Chicken-Fried Steak

Ingredients:

- 1 cup all purpose baking mix
- 1 tsp garlic powder
- 1 tsp hot paprika
- 1½ tsp salt, divided
- ½ tsp freshly ground black pepper
- 2 large eggs
- ½ cup buttermilk
- ¾ cups canola oil
- 1½ pounds London broil, cut into ¼-inch thick slices and patted dry
- 1 Tbsp fresh chopped parsley
- 1 lemon, cut into wedges

Instructions:

1.Whisk baking mix, garlic powder, paprika, 1 teaspoon salt, and pepper in a shallow bowl. Whisk eggs, buttermilk, and ½ teaspoon salt in another shallow bowl.

2.Heat oil in a large skillet until very hot. Dredge steaks in seasoned baking mix and shake off excess. Dip in egg wash, shake off excess, and dredge again in baking mix. Fry steaks in 2 batches, turning once, about 3 minutes per side.

3.Put on a warm platter and garnish with parsley and lemon wedges.

73. Slow-Cooked Pork Shoulder

Ingredients:

- 1 boneless shoulder (butt) pork roast, about 4 pounds
- ½ cup beef broth
- 2 Tbsp tamari
- ½ tsp hot pepper sauce
- 2 Tbsp red wine or cider vinegar
- 2 Tbsp sugar-free pancake syrup
- 1 tsp ground cumin

Instructions:

1.Heat oven to 325°F. Set pork in a casserole or Dutch oven with a lid. Combine broth, tamari, hot pepper sauce, vinegar, syrup, and cumin; pour over pork. Cover and bake until fork-tender, about 3 hours.

2.Set aside for about 10 minutes before slicing or shredding, and serve.

74.　Fontina-and-Prosciutto-Stuffed Veal Chops

Ingredients:

- 2 ounces fontina cheese, shredded (½ cup)
- 1 ounce prosciutto, chopped
- ¼ cup chopped fresh basil
- 4 (8-ounce) veal rib chops
- ¾ tsp salt
- ½ tsp freshly ground black pepper

Instructions:

1.Combine cheese, prosciutto, and basil in a small bowl.

2.Cut a horizontal pocket in each chop. Season chops with salt and pepper. Fill with cheese mixture; secure openings with toothpicks.

3.Prepare a medium-high-heat grill or heat a grill pan until very hot. Grill chops until they are browned and just lose their pink color throughout, about 5 minutes per side. Serve hot.

75.   Pork In Salsa Verde

Ingredients:

- 1 cup cilantro leaves and stems
- ½ cup parsley leaves and stems (chopped)
- ¼ cup extra virgin oil
- ¼ small onion (roughly chopped)
- 1 ½ tbsp. lime juice (freshly squeezed)
- 1 tsp. salt
- 1 tsp. ground pepper
- 4 pcs. of 6 oz. pork tenderloins

Directions:

1. Pre-heat grill to high and oven to 400°F at the same time.

2. Meanwhile, prepare salsa verde by pulsing all the ingredients (except for tenderloins) in a blender or food processor for about 3 minutes, until sauce turns creamy and all the herbs are finely chopped.

3. Season the pork tenderloins with generous amounts of salt and pepper. Roast in the oven for 30 minutes, then remove and transfer to grill. Let it cook for about 5 minutes on each side so pork is charred nicely.

4. Let it stand for 5 minutes. Slice into desired thickness and serve with salsa verde.

76.   Roasted Rosemary & Garlic Beef Ribs

Ingredients:

- 1 tbsp. dried rosemary (crushed)
- 3 cloves garlic (pressed or minced)
- ¾ tsp. salt
- ¼ tsp. ground pepper

- 6 lbs. (3 to 4 pcs.) small end of beef ribs (well-trimmed)

Directions:

1. Preheat oven to 350°F.

2. In a small bowl, combine the rosemary, garlic, salt and pepper. Press the mixture evenly into the beef ribs.

3. With the fat side facing up, arrange ribs in a shallow, roasting pan. If you have a meat thermometer, insert it in the thickest part of the meat without letting it rest on the fat or touch the bone.

4. Roast for 2 ½ hours or until thermometer reads 135°F for medium-rare. Transfer to a cutting board and let it stand for about 15 minutes. Slice and serve.

77.   Almond-Crusted Catfish Fingers

Ingredients:

- ¾ cup or more canola oil, for frying
- 2 large eggs
- 1 Tbsp cold water
- 1½ Tbsp Old Bay Seasoning or any Cajun spice blend
- ¾ tsp salt
- 1½ pounds catfish fillets, cut into 1½-inch-wide strips

- ¼ cup all purpose baking mix
- 1 cup almond meal
- 1 lemon, cut into wedges

Instructions:

1.Heat oil in a heavy-bottomed saucepan or Dutch oven over high heat until shimmering.

2.Lightly beat eggs in a small bowl; whisk in water and spice blend.

3.Dredge catfish in baking mix and shake off any excess. Dip into egg mixture and then dredge in almond meal. Slip catfish pieces into oil; fry 4 or 5 at a time until golden, about 2 minutes per side. Drain fish on paper towels. Serve hot with lemon wedges.

78. Baked Bluefish with Garlic and Lime

Ingredients:

- 2 Tbsp virgin olive oil, plus more for baking dish
- 2 cloves garlic, minced
- ¼ tsp red pepper flakes
- 1½ pounds bluefish fillets with skin
- Salt, to taste
- 3 limes, quartered

Instructions:

1.Grease a 9-by-13-inch baking dish with oil, and put it in the oven and heat to 425°F.

2.Combine oil, garlic, and red pepper flakes in a small bowl. Rub fillets with garlic mixture and season generously with salt to taste.

3.Using potholders, carefully remove baking dish from oven; add fillets, skin side down, and limes. Bake until fish is opaque and flakes easily, 10–12 minutes. Serve, squeezing limes over fish once they are cool enough to handle.

79.   Smoked Salmon, Cream Cheese and Tomato Stacks

Ingredients:

- 1 medium-sized tomato
- 2 tbsp. cream cheese
- 4 oz. smoked salmon (sliced into strips)
- 1 tsp. freshly ground pepper

Directions:

1.Cut off the bottom and the stem end of the tomato. Slice in half.

2.Spread cream cheese over each tomato half.

3.Top with smoked salmon. Season with pepper and serve.

80.   Baked Salmon with Mustard-Nut Crust

Ingredients:

- 4 (6-ounce) center-cut fillets of salmon
- 2 Tbsp coarse-grain Dijon mustard
- ¼ cup fine bread crumbs
- ½ cup finely ground pecans or walnuts
- 1 Tbsp chopped fresh parsley

Instructions:

1.Preheat oven to 450°F. Line a baking sheet with foil and place fillets on the sheet. Spread ½ Tbsp mustard on each fillet, covering top evenly.

2.Combine bread crumbs, nuts, and parsley in a small bowl. Divide among fillets, pressing onto mustard to form an even crust. Bake until just cooked through, about 10–15 minutes, being careful not to burn the nuts. Serve right away.

81. Roasted Fennel and Cod with Moroccan Olives

Ingredients:

- 2 fennel bulbs, trimmed and thinly sliced
- Zest of 1 lemon, save lemon
- 1 Tbsp olive oil
- ½ tsp garlic salt
- 1½ pounds cod fillets
- ½ cup black Moroccan olives, pitted
- ¼ cup chopped dill or cilantro
- ½ tsp hot paprika or ¼ tsp crushed red pepper flakes
- ¼ tsp salt
- ¼ tsp freshly ground black pepper
- 4 Tbsp unsalted butter

Instructions:

1. Preheat the oven to 400°F. Place the fennel in a 7-by-11-inch baking dish.
2. Scatter the lemon zest over the fennel, and add the olive oil and garlic salt.
3. Toss well. Bake for about 15 minutes, until the edges of the fennel start to brown.

4. Cut the zested lemon into quarters.

5. Place the fish on top of the fennel, as well as the lemon wedges, and sprinkle with the olives, dill or cilantro, paprika or chili flakes, salt, and pepper.

6. Top each piece of fish with 1 tablespoon of butter.

7. Bake for about 25 minutes, until the fish flakes when pressed with a fork.

8. Squeeze lemon juice from the lemon wedges over the fish, and serve immediately.

82.   Year-Round Barbecued Brisket

Ingredients:

- 1 (6-ounce) can tomato paste
- ⅓ cup apple cider vinegar
- 1 Tbsp chili powder
- 2 tsp onion powder
- 2 tsp garlic salt
- 1 tsp freshly ground black pepper
- 1 tsp smoked paprika
- 1 tsp cayenne pepper
- 2 Tbsp stevia

- 2 Tbsp whole grain soy flour
- 1 (5-pound) beef brisket

Instructions:

1. Place the tomato paste, vinegar, chili powder, onion powder, garlic salt, black pepper, paprika, cayenne pepper, stevia, and flour in a slow cooker.
2. Whisk to combine.
3. Remove ¼ cup of the sauce to pour over the brisket.
4. Add the brisket, and top with the removed sauce.
5. Set the slow cooker to low, and cook 9 to 10 hours, until the meat is very tender.
6. Shred or slice and serve immediately.

83.   Salmon with Rosemary

Ingredients:

- ¼ tsp salt
- 2 tsp rosemary
- 2 tsp lemon juice
- 2 tsp olive oil

- 2 Tbsp minced garlic
- ½ pound salmon fillet
- 1 small pinch pepper

Instructions:

1.Cut salmon in half.

2.In a bowl, combine the rosemary, lemon juice, olive oil, salt, garlic and pepper.

3.Use a brush to apply the mixture into the salmon.

4.Place the fillets on a broiler pan and bake in the ove at 350° F for 20 minutes. Serve.

84. Slow Cooked Pork, Cabbage and Onions

Ingredients:

- 3 pounds lean pork shoulder -- cut into bite-sized pieces
- 1 large head of cabbage -- cut into chunks 1 large onion -- cut into 1" pieces
- 1 teaspoon salt 1/2 teaspoon black pepper
- 3 each whole cloves 1/8 teaspoon nutmeg
- 6 ounces diet rite or other diet cola 1 teaspoon caraway seeds
- 6 ounces beef broth

Directions:

1. Preheat oven to 300f.
2. In an oven proof pan with a tight-fitting lid, sauté onion in bacon grease until slightly translucent.
3. Add pork cubes and sauté for 5-6 minutes or until they change colours.
4. Then add the cabbage and remaining ingredients.
5. Bring to a simmer, cover tightly with lid. Place in oven and let cook for 3-4 hours.

6. You can strain the juices out and reduce them and serve with the dish or just use a slotted spoon and serve as-is.

7. Serve in a bowl with a dollop of sour cream on top.

85.   Chorizo

Ingredients:

- 1-pound lean pork shoulder -- or tenderloin 1 tablespoon hot chili powder -- or mild
- 1/2 teaspoon salt 1/2 teaspoon black pepper
- 1 teaspoon ground cumin 1 teaspoon ground oregano
- 2 tablespoons olive oil 2 tablespoons water
- 1 teaspoon red pepper flakes 1/2 teaspoon garlic powder

Directions:

1. Roughly chop pork then process in pulses in a food processor until very fine.
2. Add remaining ingredients and pulse to blend thoroughly.
3. You want almost a pate/paste consistency.
4. Refrigerate covered overnight to allow flavors to blend.
5. Form into patties or crumbles and fry until cooked through.
6. Cook thoroughly.

86.   Kale and Sausage

Ingredients:

- 1 tube of pork sausage
- 1 bunch kale
- 1/2 stick butter

Directions:

1. Make patties out of the bulk pork sausage and start frying.
2. Wash the kale in vinegar water; shake off excess moisture.
3. Cut the kale every 1/2-inch crossway with a scissors into about one inch of boiling water in a large kettle
4. Fry the pork slowly because the kale takes about 45 minutes of simmering to get tender.
5. Either mix with pork or serve them side-by-side.
6. A delicious way to eat your greens. (If you cut the kale thin enough it's almost the texture of fettucine.

87. Italian Sausage and Greens

Ingredients:

- 1 tablespoon extra virgin olive oil
- 1 pound Italian sausage -- sweet or hot
- 1 pound kale (or mustard greens or collards or turnip greens or escarole)

- 3/4 pound mushroom minced garlic (to your taste -- we like it with a lot of garlic)
- dried red pepper flakes (also to taste) salt and pepper
- 2 cups chicken stock -- or water

Directions:

1. Cut sausage into bite size or smaller pieces, brown in olive oil. Trim and slice mushrooms.
2. When sausage is done, remove from pan and set aside. Put mushrooms in pan.
3. While mushrooms are cooking trim leaves from their stems and chop into ü inch long pieces. Roll leaves up and slice into thin strips.
4. Brown chopped up stems, then add garlic, dried red pepper and green leaves.
5. Cover and cook a few minutes
6. Add sausage and liquid and cook until greens are done.

88.   Spinach Stuffed Pork Chops

Ingredients:

- 1/4 cup chopped onion 1 box frozen spinach --
- thawed and squeezed 2 cloves garlic -- minced
- 2 tablespoons butter2 tablespoons water
- 6 pork chops -- for stuffing
- 1/4 cup olive oil 1/2 cup water

Directions:

1. Saute onion and garlic in butter until soft.

2. Add spinach and 2 tbsp water.

3. Mix well and heat through. Stuff this mixture into the pocket of the pork chop.

4. Close pock with toothpicks.

5. Heat olive oil in skillet, add chops and brown on both sides.

6. Transfer to baking dish, adding ½ cup water.

7. Bake for 1.5 hours or until chops are tender.

89.　Savory Rosemary Pork

Ingredients:

- 4 pork cutlets -- thinly sliced 1 clove garlic -- to taste
- 2 teaspoons rosemary -- to taste salt -- to taste
- black pepper -- to taste
- 2 tablespoons heavy cream
- 1 tablespoon sour cream
- 2 large mushrooms olive oil

Directions:

1. Sautee pork and mushrooms and seasonings in olive oil over medium heat until lightly browned.

2. Turn heat to low, add cream and sour cream stir continuously until warm.

3. Do not let this boil.

90.   Paprika Pork Chops

Ingredients:

- 4 pork chops 3 tablespoons paprika -- (3 to 4)
- salt and pepper
- 1 tablespoon Mrs. Dash
- 1/2 cup sour cream
- 1/2 cup heavy cream
- 1/3 cup water
- 3 egg yolks 3 slices bacon -- diced
- 1/4 cup butter

Directions:

1. Saute the bacon in skillet until golden brown, remove.
2. Saute pork chops on both sides in bacon fat.
3. When chops are browned on both sides, remove.
4. To the pan add salt and pepper, paprika, Mrs. Dash, and water.
5. Scrape the pan drippings to release into mixture.
6. Allow to reduce by 1/3 over low heat, just below a boil.
7. Beat egg yolks, add a bit of the mixture into the egg yolks and whisk........do not allow yolks to scramble......then add to mixture.

8. Remove from heat...whiskin butter and sour cream.Add chops to reheat.

9. Serve with low carb aktins noodles (egg whites beaten, salt, and egg yolks folded in.........spread on a greased cookie sheet and baked for 10 min 350 degrees, then sliced into strips when cool.

91.   Smothered Pork Loin Chops

Ingredients:

- 1 thick cut pork loin chops -- (4 1/2")
- 1 tablespoon flour
- 1 tablespoon butter meat tenderizer
- fresh cracked pepper 1 cup chicken stock1 shallot -- minced
- 1 tablespoon parsley
- 1/2 cup whipping cream
- 8 ounces fresh mushrooms -- sliced
- 4 tablespoons olive oil

Directions:

1. Season pork with tenderizer and pepper.
2. In a fry pan heat 1 T olive oil and saute the shallot till tender.
3. Add butter to pan and combine flour to make a roux, cook for 3 minutes to remove flour taste.
4. Add in chicken stock and cook till thickened slightly. In a separate pan add 3 T olive oil and fry the pork till cooked through.
5. Add mushrooms to the sauce and cook till tender, add the cream and reduce the sauce till thick and bubbly.
6. Tossing the parsley and serve over the pork loins.

92.   Juicy Pork Tenderloin

Ingredients:

- 2 pounds pork tenderloin
- 1/4 cup vermouth
- 2 cloves garlic -- minced
- 3 tablespoons artificial
- sweetener 1 teaspoon Worcestershire sauce
- 1/2 teaspoon salt
- 1/2 teaspoon red pepper
- 3 tablespoons sugar free ketchup
- 2 teaspoons rosemary --fresh, finely chopped

Directions:

1. Cut tenderloin into 2 strips, lengthwise.
2. Mix marinade and rub into meat.Refrigerate for 2-4 hours.
3. Place on roasting rack in pan.
4. Roast for 35-45 mins or until juices run clear.
5. Let stand 10 minutes, cut into slices and pour pan juices over meat.

93. Pork Casserole

Ingredients:

- 12 ounces fresh mushrooms
- 1/4 cup chopped onion
- 3 tablespoons butter 1 pound pork browned and drained
- 1 package frozen spinach – thawed
- 1 pinch seasoning
- 3/4 cup heavy cream
- 2 eggs
- 1 cup Swiss cheese

Directions:

1. Preheat oven to 375 and grease casserole dish with butter.
2. In a bowl, combine cream, egg, and the egg yolks.
3. Pour cream/egg mixture over everything else, browned and simmering.
4. Bake 30 minutes.

94. Salisbury Steak

Ingredients:

- 1 pound ground beef
- 1/3 cup dry bread crumbs
- 1/2 teaspoon salt
- 1/4 teaspoon pepper
- 1 egg

- 1/4 cup sliced onion
- 10 1/2 ounces beef broth -- condensed
- 4 ounces mushroom stems and pieces -- drained
- 3/4 teaspoon Guar gum

Directions:

1. Mix ground beef, bread crumbs, salt & pepper and egg;shape into 4 oval patties, each about 3/4inch thick.
2. Cook patties over medium heat, turning occasionally, until brown, about 10 minutes; drain.
3. Add onion, broth & mushrooms.
4. Heat toboiling; reduce heat. Cover & simmer until beef is done,about 10 minutes.
5. Remove patties; keep warm.
6. Heat onion mixture to a boil. Sprinkle guar gum over mixture; stir in.
7. Heat for a couple of minutes and will start to thicken. If too thick add some water to desired consistency (I add 1/2 can of water to make more gravy & cut down on the salty taste).

95.   Round Steak Rollups

Ingredients:

- 2 Round Steaks 16 ounces pork sausage --any brand
- 2 large bell peppers -- sliced in thin strips
- 1 Medium onion -- sliced in thin strips
- 1/4 Cup pepper jack cheese
- Seasoning to Taste Lemon Pepper To Taste

Directions:

1. Preheat oven to 350 degrees.
2. Put round steak on chopping board and pound it with any large utensil Season each steak on both sides.
3. Cover each steak with the 1/4 of the pork sausage, then add a palm full of peppers and onions and 1/8 cup of pepper jack to each.
4. Roll the steak and put tooth picks into the steak to hold it shut. Bake in oven from 25 to 30 minutes, making sure that pork is cooked through.

96. Roast Beef Melt

Ingredients:

- 2 slices leftover roast beef
- 2 green pepper slices -- cut
- in 2 inch pieces
- 3 mushrooms -- sliced
- 2 onion slice -- cut in 2 inch
- pieces1 tablespoon butter
- 2 tablespoons LC Ranch

Dressing

- Mozzarella cheese to cover

Directions:

The quantities are approximate - add to your liking. Place roast beef on a heat proof plate or pan. Saute vegetables in butter until tender-crisp and place on top of beef. Spread dressing over the vegetables and top with mozzarella cheese. Broil until cheese is hot and bubbly. This is a quick and easy way to use up leftover roast.

97.   Red Hot Sirloin

Ingredients:

- 1 pound Beef top sirloin
- 1/2 cup FRANK"S Red Hot
- 3 tablespoons butter
- Salt a Fresh cracked pepper

Directions:

1. Season the sirloin with salt and pepper and grill till desired doneness.
2. In a saucepan over low heat melt butter and hot sauce together until mixture is hot and blended.
3. Pour directly over hot sirloin and serve.

Soups & Salads

98.   Blue Cheese and Bacon Soup

Ingredients:

- 6 strips of bacon
- 3 tbsp.butter

- 2 cups button, cremini, Portobello, or shitake mushrooms (sliced)
- 2 leeks (halved lengthwise then chopped)
- 1 ½ cups cauliflower florets
- 29 oz. chicken broth
- ½ cup of water
- 5 oz. blue cheese (crumbled)

Directions:

1. Heat a skillet over medium-high heat. Cook 3 strips of bacon until crispy on one side. Turn the bacon over and cook until crispy all over. Remove from pan and place on a plate with paper towels to remove any excess fat.

2. Do the same with the remaining bacon strips. Set aside and let it cool.

3. Meanwhile, put butter in a soup pot and let it melt over medium heat. Add the mushrooms, leek and cauliflower. Cover pot and let it cook for 5 minutes; stir vegetables occasionally.

4. Add chicken broth and water. Bring soup to a boil, leaving pot uncovered.

5. Lower heat and cover pot. Let soup simmer for 10 minutes or until vegetables turn very tender.

6. Puree the soup in batches using a food processor or a blender until smooth. On the last batch of soup, add blue cheese and puree.

7. Put the soup back in pot and heat if necessary.

8. Take cooked bacon and crumble. Serve the soup hot and sprinkle with crumbled bacon.

99.   Spicy Tuna Steak Salad

Ingredients:

- 2 tbsp. lemon zest
- 2 tsp. coriander (ground)
- 2 tsp. salt
- 1 ½ tsp. black pepper (freshly ground)
- 1 ½ tsp. ginger (ground)
- ½ tsp. cinnamon
- 1 ½ lbs. tuna (4 steaks)
- 4 tbsp. extra virgin olive oil
- 2 tps. balsamic vinegar
- 2 cups arugula

Directions:

1. In a small bowl, combine the lemon zest, coriander, salt, pepper, ginger and cinnamon. Add 2 tablespoons of the olive oil and stir thoroughly. Rub the mixture on the tuna steaks.

2. In a large skillet, heat 1 tbsp. of oil over high heat. Sauté the tuna steaks for 2-3 minutes, turn and cook for another 2-3 minutes until tuna is just cooked through.

3. Meanwhile, on a separate small bowl, place the balsamic vinegar and whisk in 1 tablespoon (or more, if desired) of olive oil. Add salt and pepper and continue to whisk mixture until a slightly thick dressing is made.

4. Toss arugula with the dressing until evenly coated.

5. Slice the tuna into ¼-inch pieces and serve over salad greens.

100.   Athenian Salad

Ingredients:

- 6 Tbsp extra-virgin olive oil
- 1 clove garlic, finely minced
- 1½ tsp dried oregano, crumbled, or 1 Tbsp fresh oregano, chopped
- ½ tsp salt

- ¼ tsp freshly ground black pepper
- 2 Tbsp + 1 tsp freshly squeezed lemon juice
- ½ small red onion, thinly sliced
- 1½ medium cucumbers, peeled, halved lengthwise, seeded, and thinly sliced
- 1 medium green bell pepper, stemmed, ribs removed, and thinly sliced
- ½ cup pitted quartered kalamata or other black olives
- 12 cherry tomatoes, quartered
- ½ cup crumbled feta cheese

Instructions:

1.Whisk together oil, garlic, oregano, salt and pepper in a small bowl; whisk in lemon juice.

2.Put onion, cucumbers, bell pepper, and olives in a bowl and toss with the dressing. Arrange on a large platter or four individual plates, top with tomatoes and cheese, and serve.

101.   Caprese Salad

Ingredients:

- 1 pound fresh mozzarella, cut into ¼-inch slices
- 4 medium tomatoes, cored and cut into ¼-inch slices
- ¼ cup extra-virgin olive oil
- 4 tsp red wine vinegar
- 1 tsp granular sugar substitute
- ½ tsp salt
- ¼ tsp freshly ground black pepper
- 6 basil leaves, cut into thin strips

Instructions:

1. Arrange mozzarella and tomatoes on a platter, alternating and overlapping the slices decoratively.
2. Whisk together oil, vinegar, sugar substitute, salt, and pepper in a small bowl.
3. Drizzle over cheese and tomatoes, and then scatter basil on top.

102.   Old Bay Shrimp Salad

Ingredients:

- 1 pound frozen cooked small shrimp, defrosted
- 1 cup cauliflower florets, chopped
- 2 celery stalks, thinly sliced
- ¾ cup mayonnaise

- 2 scallions, thinly sliced
- 1 Tbsp Old Bay seasoning or seasoning salt
- 1 head Bibb lettuce, broken into 12 leaves

Instructions:

1. Drain the shrimp on paper towels or a kitchen towel to be sure they are dry.
2. Transfer to a bowl along with the cauliflower, celery, mayonnaise, scallions, and Old Bay.
3. Stir well.
4. Set the leaves out on salad plates and divide the salad among the 12 leaves and serve immediately

103. Watercress Bacon Salad with Ranch Dressing

Ingredients:

- ½ pound watercress
- ½ pound baby spinach

- 2 tomatoes, chopped
- 1 ripe Hass avocado, diced
- 4 slices cooked bacon, crumbled

Ranch Dressing

- ½ cup mayonnaise
- 2 Tbsp canned coconut milk or heavy cream
- 1 tsp apple cider vinegar
- ½ tsp onion powder
- ½ tsp garlic salt
- 1 Tbsp chopped fresh dill or flat-leaf parsley
- ¼ tsp freshly ground black pepper

Instructions:

1.Combine the watercress and spinach, tossing well. Put equally on four plates and top with the tomatoes, avocado, and bacon.

2.Place the mayonnaise, coconut milk or heavy cream, vinegar, onion powder, garlic salt, dill or parsley, and black pepper in a large bowl.

3.Whisk well to combine. Serve over the salad.

104. Chicken, Mushrooom And Bok Choy Soup

Ingredients:

- 43.5 oz chicken broth
- 3 tbsp. ginger root, shopped finely
- 12 oz. shiitake mushrooms

- 4 tbsp. Nam Pla fish sauce
- 2 tbsp. tamari
- 1 tbsp. sesame oil
- 1/8 tsp. red pepper flakes (crushed)
- 10 oz. chicken (breast part, shredded)
- ¾ lbs. bok choy (sliced)
- 4 tsp. rice vinegar (unsweetened)
- 2 medium-sized green onions (sliced thinly)

Directions:

1. In a large pot, pour in chicken broth and add ginger and mushrooms. Bring to a boil. Lower the heat and let it simmer for 3 minutes.

2. Add the Nam Pla fish sauce, tamari, sesame oil and pepper flakes. Let it simmer for 2 more minutes.

3. Add the shredded chicken and bok choy, then let it simmer for another 2 minutes.

4. Stir in the rice vinegar and add salt and pepper to taste.

5. Remove from heat and serve garnished with green onion slices.

105. Chicken Bacon Club Salad

Ingredients:

- 4 boneless skinless chicken breasts
- 1 Cup Mayo
- 6 slices bacon
- 2 Cups shredded cheddar cheese

Directions:

1. Cook bacon until crisp, then crumble.
2. Cube chicken breast and cook thoroughly.
3. Mix all ingredients together.

4. Spared into a 8" cake pan.
5. Bake for about 15 minutes.
6. Serve on top of a bed of lettuce. Top with black olives if you like.

106. Chicken Taco Salad

Ingredients:

- 4 chicken breast – boil, then shred with fork
- Olive Oil Cumin
- Chili Powder 1 Can Rotel tomatoes with green chilis
- 1 Large yellow onion – diced 1 Head Iceberg lettuce
- 1 Can black olives Shredded cheddar cheese
- Sour Cream Guacamole (optional)Homemade Salsa:
- 1 large can peeled tomatoes 1 small bunch cilantro
- 1 medium/large onion garlic salt

Directions:

1. In a large skillet, pour about 2 Tblsp olive oil and turn up to med/high heat. Sautee about ¼ of the onions.
2. Add the shredded chicken, cumin and chili powder and Rotel.
3. Simmer for approximately 20 minutes, stirring occasionally. Meanwhile, shred lettuce and place in bowls.
4. When Chicken mixture is done, place a heaping on top of the lettuce and cover with cheese, olives, sour cream, the remaining onions.
5. Combine salsa ingredients in blender.
6. Add to salad this will be used as your dressing.

107. Easy Egg Plant Salad

Ingredients:

- 1 large eggplant – cut
- ½" pieces 1 large onion – cut
- ½" pieces, (red, white, yellow, spanish)
- 1 can pitted black olives – diced small
- 1 small jar spanish olives diced into small pieces
- ¼ cup cider vinegar – more to taste
- 1 quart tomato sauce – whatever low carb brand you use

Directions:

1. Mix all chopped ingredients and add the vinegar. Toss well to mix the vinegar with the mixed veggies. Let set a few minutes and toss again. Add the tomato sauce and mix again.

2. Add red pepper and black to taste (1/2 tsp red is hot). Mix one more time before placing in a 4 qt.

3. Corning ware pot. Bake in the oven at 325`F for about 1 hour (1 ½ hours is mushy)

4. Let cool to room temperature, toss and refigerate before serving (sandwich spread, appetizer, main course with chicken,pork or beef).

5. recipe is about 15 minutes, has a very unique taste that satisfies the appetite.

108. Chilled Seafood Bisque

Ingredients:

- 1 tbsp. butter (unsalted)
- 1/3 cup medium-sized white onion (chopped)
- 27 oz. clam juice
- ¾ cup heavy cream
- 1/8 tbsp. thyme
- 6 pcs. Large shrimps (cooked and diced)

Directions:

1. Place a saucepan over medium-low heat and melt butter. Cook onions for 3 to 4 minutes, or until they turn translucent.

2. Pour in the clam juice and bring to a boil. Reduce heat slightly, cook for 5 minutes and let it cool.

3. Meanwhile, in a separate small saucepan, mix in cream and thyme and bring to a boil. Reduce heat slightly and cook for 5 to 7 minutes, or until mixture is reduced to just about half a cup. Discard thyme and let it cool.

4. Stir in reduced cream to the clam juice and puree mixture in batches using a food processor or blender until smooth.

5. Place in an airtight container and chill in the fridge until just cool or cold, depending on your preference.

6. Serve in four bowls then top with diced shrimps. Garnish with a small sprig of thyme if desired.

109.   Creamy Spinach Soup

Ingredients:

- 2 tbsp. butter (unsalted)
- 1 pc. of small onion (chopped finely)
- 1 tsp. garlic (chopped)
- 43 ½ oz. chicken broth
- 20 oz. frozen chopped spinach (thawed)
- 2 cups heavy cream
- 1/2tsp. ground nutmeg

Directions:

1. Place a large stockpot over medium heat and melt butter. Sauté onions for about 4 minutes or until they turn soft. Add in the garlic and sauté for about 30 seconds until aroma is released.

2. Add the broth and spinach then let it simmer for around 5 minutes. Remove from heat.

3. Puree the soup in batches using a food processor or a blender until smooth. Put soup back in the pot and add the cream. Cook over low heat until soup is warm.

4. Stir in nutmeg and remove from heat. Season with salt and pepper to taste and serve.

110. Tarragon Shrimp Salad

Ingredients:

- ¼ cup mayonnaise
- 2 tbsp. Dijon mustard
- 2 tbsp. dried capers
- 1 tbsp. fresh parsley (chopped)
- 1 tsp. fresh tarragon (chopped)
- 2 anchovy fillets (oil-packed, mashed)
- 1 ½ lbs. medium-sized shrimps (deveined, cooked and shelled)

Directions:

1. Whisk together all ingredients except for the shrimp in a large serving bowl. Mix well until evenly combined. Add salt and pepper to taste.

2. Add the shrimp and toss well so that shrimp is evenly coated. Serve immediately

111.   Turkey Cobb Salad with Italian Dressing

Ingredients:

For Salad:

- 6 bacon strips
- 6 cups Romaine lettuce (shredded)
- 2 large eggs (hard-boiled, peeled, diced)
- 2 cups turkey (cooked, chopped)
- 1 hass avocado (cubed)
- 2 small tomatoes (cored, chopped)
- ¾ cup blue cheese (crumbled)

For Italian Dressing:

- ½ cup extra virgin olive oil
- 1 medium clove of garlic (pressed or finely minced)
- 2 tbsp. red wine vinegar
- 1 ½ tbsp. fresh parsley (minced)
- 1 tbsp. lemon juice (freshly squeezed)
- ½ tbsp. fresh basil (minced)
- 1 tsp. dried oregano
- ¼ tsp. red pepper flakes

- ½ tsp. granular sugar substitute (sucralose)
- 1/8 tsp. salt
- 1/8 tsp. freshly ground pepper.

Directions:

1. First prepare the dressing by combining all ingredients with a blender. Set aside or refrigerate if desired.

2. On a skillet, cook bacon over medium-high heat until crispy. Drain off excess fat with a paper towel and chop coarsely or crumble with hands when cool enough. Set aside.

3. In a large bowl, toss the Romaine lettuce with around 3 tablespoons of the Italian dressing. Place lettuce on a large serving platter.

4. Place the remaining salad ingredients over the lettuce, arranging them in vertical stripes if you wish.

5. Drizzle with remaining Italian dressing and serve immediately.

112.   Guacamole Soup

Ingredients:

- 2 medium-sized green onions (cut into 1-in pcs)
- ½ cup fresh cilantro leaves
- 1 pc. fresh jalapeno (seeded, chopped coarsely)
- 2 hass avocado (peeled, pitted, chopped coarsely)
- 14 ½ oz. chicken broth
- ½ cup tomato juice
- ¼ cup lemon juice

Directions:

1. Using a food processor, pulse onions, cilantro leaves and jalapeno until mixture is finely chopped.

2. Add avocado, broth, tomato juice and lemon juice. Pulse until mixture is smooth. Season with salt, and add Tabasco if desired.

3. Refrigerate for an hour and serve chilled. If desired, you may prepare the soup 8 hours ahead and let it chill overnight to allow flavors to blend well.

113. Quick Bouillabaisse

Ingredients:

- ¼ cup extra virgin olive oil
- 2 stalks of celery (chopped)
- ½ small fennel bulb (chopped)
- ½ small onion (chopped)
- 1 garlic clove (sliced thinly)
- 29 oz. chicken broth
- 14 ½ oz. water
- 3 tbsp. orange zest (or 3 strips of 2 x ½ in orange peel)
- 2 tbsp. tomato paste
- ½ tsp. fennel seeds
- ½ tsp. dried tarragon
- 20 mussels (washed and beards pulled off)
- 1 ½ lbs. fish fillets (white fish like snapper, cod, or monk fish; cut into 2 pieces)
- 1 lb. medium-sized shrimps (shelled)
- ¼ cup fresh parsley (chopped)

Directions:

1.In a large saucepot, heat the olive oil over medium heat. Add the celery, fennel and onion then cook for around 5 minutes, until they soften. Add the garlic and cook for another minute.

2.Pour in the chicken broth and water. Add the orange zest (or peel), tomato paste, fennel seeds and tarragon. Bring to a boil.

3.Reduce the heat and add the mussels. Cover pot and cook for 10 minutes.

4.Add the fish fillet. Wait for 5 minutes then add the shrimp. Cook for 35 more minutes. Season with salt and freshly ground pepper to taste. 5.Divide in serving bowls. Make sure that you discard any unopened mussels, if any. Garnish with parsley and serve hot.

114. Broccoli, Olives, & Egg Salad

Ingredients:

- Fresh broccoli florets Boiled eggs
- Green olives Red Onion
- Mayonnaise Black Pepper
- Paprika Salt

Directions:

1. Quantities of everything according to taste.
2. I would use I bunch broccoli, 3 eggs chopped in large pieces, ½ cup olives, ½ large red onion chopped.

3. The rest of the ingredients really depend on your preferences, but black pepper really makes this salad.
4. Mix everything together and coat well with mayo.
5. Chill and serve.

115.   Bruschetta Style Tomato Turkey Salad

Ingredients:

- 1 cup ground turkey 1 cup mixed lettuce
- 1 tomato
- 4 or 5 kalamata olives
- salt pepper
- 1 or 2 T olive oil
- 1 tsp crushed garlic 1 tsp basil paste (or a few leaves of finely chopped fresh basil)

Directions:

1. Dice the tomato and place in a small bowl.
2. Add chopped olives, olive oil, garlic, basil, and salt and pepper to taste.
3. Brown the turkey mince in a saucepan.
4. Add the tomato mix to the turkey and mix together.
5. Serve over a bed of mixed lettuce.

116.   Caulif-broccoli salad

Ingredients:

- 1 lg head cauliflower
- 1 lg bunch broccoli
- 1 sm onion (or 4 green ones)
- 1 pkg froz peas (or pea pods)
- 2 cups mayo
- 1 cup sour cream 1 tsp garlic powder

Directions:

1. Mix mayo, sour cream and garlic powder in a small bowl.
2. Break caulif and broccoli into bite sized florets.
3. Add onion.
4. Toss sauce with broccoli, cauliflower and onion.
5. Add peas last (if using pods, cut into ¼ inch pieces). Refrigerate at least 4 hours or overnight.

117.   Jalapeño Cheddar Broccoli Soup

Ingredients:

- 3 Tbsp olive oil
- 1 head broccoli, cut into florets
- 6 jalapeños, seeded and diced
- ½ onion, chopped
- 1 tsp salt
- ½ tsp curry powder or ground turmeric
- ½ tsp freshly ground black pepper
- 2 Tbsp flour
- 1 quart bone broth, or unsalted chicken or beef broth

- ¼ cup heavy cream
- 1 Tbsp hot sauce
- 4 slices (4 ounces) cheddar cheese

Instructions:

1. Warm the olive oil in a stockpot.
2. Add the broccoli, jalapeños, onion, salt, curry powder or turmeric, and pepper; cook 5 to 6 minutes, stirring often, until the onion begins to brown.
3. Sprinkle with the flour and cook 1 minute more, stirring often, until the flour coats the vegetables. Add the broth and cover.
4. Cook for 15 minutes.
5. Using an immersion blender, blend until smooth. Stir in the heavy cream and hot sauce.
6. Set the oven to broil. Transfer the soup to four oven-safe bowls and top each with one a slice of cheese.
7. Place under the broiler for 3 minutes, until the cheese is melted and bubbly. Serve immediately.

118. Cauliflower Bisque

Ingredients:

- 3 tablespoons unsalted butter
- 1 head cauliflower, cut into florets
- 4 garlic cloves, chopped
- ½ teaspoon salt
- ½ teaspoon freshly grated nutmeg
- ¼ teaspoon freshly ground black pepper
- 1 quart basic bone broth or unsalted chicken or vegetable broth
- 1 tablespoon lemon juice
- ½ cup heavy cream or canned coconut milk

- 4 teaspoons olive oil
- ½ red bell pepper, minced

Instructions:

1. Put the butter in a large stockpot, and warm over medium heat, about 1 minute, until the butter foams.
2. Add the cauliflower, garlic, salt, nutmeg, and pepper; cook 5 to 6 minutes, stirring often, until the garlic begins to brown.
3. Add the broth and lemon juice and cover.
4. Cook 15 to 20 minutes, until the cauliflower is fork tender.
5. Using an immersion blender, blend until smooth.
6. Stir in the heavy cream or coconut milk.
7. Spoon into 4 bowls, garnish each serving with the olive oil and bell pepper, and serve immediately.

119. Spicy Korean Soup with Scallions

Ingredients:

- 1 pound flank steak
- ½ tsp freshly ground black pepper
- 3 Tbsp sesame oil
- 10 ounces mushrooms, such as button, shiitake, or cremini
- 8 scallions, thinly sliced
- 4 garlic cloves, minced
- 2 tsp crushed red pepper flakes
- ¼ tsp salt

- 2 Tbsp soy sauce or tamari
- 2 Tbsp apple cider vinegar
- 1 quart beef broth

Instructions:

1. Place the flank steak in a large stockpot, and cover with water.
2. Add the black pepper and bring to a boil over high heat. Reduce the heat to low and simmer, covered, for 2 hours, until the meat is very tender.
3. Drain, discarding the liquid, and let the beef cool. Use a fork to shred the meat.
4. Wash and dry the stockpot. Warm the oil in the stockpot over medium-low heat.
5. Add the mushrooms, scallions, garlic, red pepper flakes, and salt, and cook for about 3 minutes, stirring often, until fragrant.
6. Add the shredded beef, soy sauce or tamari, vinegar, and broth.
7. Bring to a simmer and cook for 5 minutes, until the mushrooms are tender.
8. Serve immediately.

120. Caesar Salad

Ingredients:

- 1 head Romaine lettuce (torn into bite-size pcs.)
- 7 tbsp. parmesan cheese (grated)
- ¼ cup mayonnaise
- 1 tbsp. fresh lemon juice
- 1 tbsp. extra virgin olive oil
- 1 tbsp. anchovy paste
- 1 ½ tsp. Worcestershire sauce
- 1 tsp. Dijon mustard
- 1 tsp. garlic (minced finely)
- ¼ tsp. salt
- ¼ tsp. freshly ground black pepper
- 1/8 tbsp. Tabasco (optional)
- 8 canned anchovies (drained, optional)

Directions:

1. Place lettuce and 4 tablespoons of the cheese in a large bowl and toss.

2. To make dressing, combine all remaining ingredients, except for anchovies, in a small bowl.

3. Toss in mixture with the lettuce until the dressing is evenly distributed.

4.Serve in four separate plates and top with 2 anchovies each, if desired.

121.   Canned Tuna And Artichoke Salad

Ingredients:

- 4 oz. canned tuna
- 3 pcs. Marinated artichoke hearts (chopped)
- 2 tbsp. mayonnaise
- 2 cups Romaine lettuce (shredded)

Directions:

1.Drain canned tuna. Place tuna in a mixing bowl and combine with artichoke and mayonnaise. Season with salt and ground pepper.

2.Assemble lettuce on a plate. Top with tuna mixture and serve.

122. Chef Salad With Blue Cheese Dressing

Ingredients:

For Salad

- 1 strip of bacon
- 6 oz. chicken breast
- 1 cup mixed greens
- ½ hass avocado (sliced)
- ½ medium-sized tomato (chopped)
- ¼ cup Monterey Jack cheese (diced)

For Blue Cheese Dressing:

- 4 oz. blue cheese (crumbled)
- ½ cup sour cream
- ½ cup mayonnaise
- 1/3 cup heavy cream
- 1 tbsp. fresh lemon juice
- ½ tsp. Dijon mustard
- ½ tsp. freshly ground pepper

Directions:

1.Cook bacon until crispy on a skillet over medium-high heat. Drain off excess fat on a paper towel and let it stand for a while until cool enough to crumble. Set aside.

2.Poach the chicken in water set over medium heat. Cook for around 8 minutes, until meat turns white. Remove chicken from water and chop into bitesized pieces. Sprinkle with salt and pepper to taste.

3.Prepare Blue Cheese Dressing by combining the ingredients in a medium bowl. Use a fork to break up the cheese and mash the mixture until combined well.

4.Place salad greens, avocado, tomato and Monterey Jack cheese in the same bowl and toss well until evenly coated with dressing. Sprinkle with crumbled bacon and serve.

123.   Salsa Verde Chicken Soup

Ingredients:

- 4 chicken breasts, on the bone, skin intact (about 1½ pounds)
- ½ tsp salt
- ½ tsp mild chili powder
- ¼ tsp freshly ground black pepper
- 2 Tbsp olive oil
- ½ red or white onion, minced
- 2 cups cauliflower florets
- 2 cups fresh cilantro leaves and stems, chopped and divided

- 4 garlic cloves
- 1 quart unsalted chicken broth
- ½ cup commercial salsa verde
- ¼ cup sour cream

Instructions:

1. Sprinkle the chicken with the salt, chili powder, and pepper. Warm the oil in a stockpot over medium heat.
2. Add the chicken and cook for 8 minutes, turning a few times, until the chicken is well browned. Transfer the chicken to a plate.
3. Add the onion, cauliflower, half the cilantro, and the garlic, cooking 5 to 6 minutes more, until the vegetables soften.
4. Return the chicken to the stockpot, and cover with the broth.
5. Bring to a simmer and cook 20 to 25 minutes, until the chicken is cooked through.
6. Remove the skin and bones.
7. Shred the chicken.
8. Return it to the soup, and top with the salsa verde and the remaining cilantro.
9. Serve with the sour cream.

124. Chicken Vegetable Soup

Ingredients:

- 1 pound skinless chicken breasts
- ½ cup chopped carrots
- ¼ cup chopped celery
- ¼ cup chopped onion
- Salt and pepper

Instructions:

1. Cook chicken breasts in a pot with 2½ cups of water over medium heat for 20 minutes.

2. Remove the chicken from the broth and cut into strips.

3. Put the chicken strips back into the pot with the broth.

4. Season with salt and pepper.

5. Add the rest of the ingredients.

6. Cook for about 1 hour more or until vegetables are done.

125. Thai Coconut-Shrimp Soup

Ingredients:

- 3 cups chicken broth
- 1 (13½-ounce) can unsweetened coconut milk
- 1 (1-inch) piece fresh ginger, peeled, cut into ⅛-inch slices
- 2 Tbsp fish sauce (nam pla or nuoc nam)
- 1 jalapeño, finely chopped
- 1 Tbsp freshly grated lime zest

- 1 tsp granular sugar substitute
- 1 pound medium shrimp, peeled and deveined
- 4 ounces button mushrooms, cut into ¼-inch slices (optional)
- 2 scallions, thinly sliced
- ¼ cup chopped fresh cilantro
- 1 Tbsp fresh lime juice

Instructions:

1. Combine first seven ingredients in a soup pot over medium-low heat. Bring to a low boil and simmer for 10 minutes.

2. Add shrimp and mushrooms, if using; simmer until shrimp are cooked through, 3 to 5 minutes.

3.Remove and discard ginger.

4.Stir in the remaining 3 ingredients and serve.

126. Chinese Hot-and-Sour Soup

Ingredients:

- ⅓ cup unseasoned, unsweetened rice vinegar
- 1 Tbsp Dixie Carb Counters Thick-It-Up low-carb thickener
- 1 tsp canola oil

- 1 clove garlic, finely chopped
- ½ cup button mushrooms, thinly sliced
- 4 cups chicken broth
- 1 (10½-ounce) package firm tofu, cut into ¼-inch dice
- 2 Tbsp tamari
- ½ tsp red pepper flakes
- 1 tsp dark (toasted) sesame oil

Instructions:

1.Whisk together vinegar and thickener in a small bowl; set aside.

2.Heat canola oil in a soup pot over medium-high heat. Add garlic and sauté until fragrant, about 30 seconds. Add mushrooms and sauté until slightly soft, about 3 minutes.

3.Add broth, tofu, tamari, and pepper flakes; cover and simmer until flavors blend, 5 to 7 minutes. Stir in vinegar mixture and simmer until soup thickens, about 1 minute. Add sesame oil just before serving.

127.   Creamy Cheddar Cheese Soup

Ingredients:

- 1 Tbsp butter
- 1 shallot, minced
- 2½ cups vegetable broth

- 1 Tbsp Dixie Carb Counters Thick-It-Up low-carb thickener
- 1½ cups half-and-half
- 8 ounces Cheddar cheese, shredded (2 cups)
- 2 tsp hot paprika
- ½ tsp salt

Instructions:

1. Melt butter in a saucepan.
2. Add shallot and sauté until soft, about 3 minutes.
3. Add broth and bring to a simmer.
4. Whisk in thickener; cook until mixture thickens, about 2 minutes.
5. Add half-and-half and simmer, stirring occasionally, until hot.
6. Slowly whisk in cheese until melted and thoroughly combined.
7. Stir in paprika and salt and serve.

128. Cream of Broccoli Soup

Ingredients:

- 4 cups vegetable or chicken broth
- 1 tsp salt
- ¼ tsp freshly ground black pepper

- 1 pound broccoli, cut into florets; stems peeled and cut into 1-inch pieces
- 1 Tbsp Dixie Carb Counters Thick-It-Up low-carb thickener
- 1 cup heavy cream

Instructions:

1. Combine broth, salt, and pepper in a soup pot over medium-high heat; bring to a boil.
2. Add broccoli, reduce the heat to medium-low, and simmer until tender, about 15 minutes.
3. Transfer soup to a blender.
4. Blend at low speed to purée. Return soup to the pot; bring back to a simmer over medium-high heat.
5. Whisk in thickener and cream; simmer, whisking occasionally, until thick and hot, about 5 minutes.
6. Serve hot or refrigerate in an airtight container for up to 3 days.
7. Reheat before serving.

129. Cold Roasted Tomato Soup

Ingredients:

- 3 pounds fresh plum tomatoes, halved lengthwise
- 1 small yellow onion, peeled and quartered
- 3 Tbsp extra-virgin olive oil
- 3 cloves garlic, peeled
- 1½ tsp salt
- ½ tsp freshly ground black pepper
- 4 cups chicken broth
- 6 Tbsp thinly sliced fresh basil

Instructions:

1. Heat oven to 450°F. Line a jelly-roll pan with parchment paper or foil.

2. Combine tomatoes, onion, oil, garlic, salt, and pepper in a mixing bowl; toss to coat. Transfer ingredients to the pan, making sure to include all of the liquid and arranging tomatoes cut side down in a single layer.

3. Roast until tomato skins are puckered and browned, about 20 minutes, rotating pan once halfway through. Let cool.

4. Add garlic and roasted vegetables and any juices to a blender.

5. Holding down blender lid firmly with a folded kitchen towel, blend at low speed until slightly chunky (you may have to work in batches).

6. Add broth and pulse once to combine.

5. Refrigerate until ready to serve or at least 1 hour. Serve, topped with basil.

130. Shaved Fennel Salad with Lemon Dressing

Ingredients:

- ¼ pound green beans, cut into 1½-inch pieces
- ¼ cup extra-virgin olive oil
- 3 Tbsp freshly squeezed lemon juice
- 1 tsp freshly grated lemon zest
- 1 tsp red wine vinegar
- ½ tsp salt
- ½ tsp freshly ground black pepper
- ¼ tsp granular sugar substitute
- 2 medium fennel bulbs, cored, quartered lengthwise, and thinly sliced crosswise
- 2 Tbsp chopped fresh basil

Instructions:

1. In a pot, bBring well-salted water to a boil over high heat. Add green beans and cook for about 4 minutes. Drain; set aside.

2. Combine oil, lemon juice, lemon zest, vinegar, salt, pepper, and sugar substitute in a salad bowl.

3. Add green beans, fennel, and basil and combine; cover and refrigerate at least 30 minutes but no more than 3 hours to let flavors blend.

4. Stir gently before serving.

131. Cucumber-Dill Salad

Ingredients:

- ½ cup white wine vinegar
- ¼ cup chopped fresh dill
- 2 tsp granular sugar substitute
- 1 tsp salt
- 4 medium cucumbers, thinly sliced

Instructions:

1. Combine vinegar, dill, sugar substitute, and salt in a medium bowl.

2. Add cucumbers and toss gently to coat.

3. Refrigerate 30 minutes to let flavors blend.

4. Drain excess liquid before serving.

132. Slaw with Vinegar Dressing

Ingredients:

- ⅓ cup white or red wine vinegar
- 1 Tbsp Dijon mustard
- 1 clove garlic, minced
- ⅓ cup extra-virgin olive oil

- ¼ cup chopped fresh parsley
- 4 small scallions, thinly sliced
- ½ tsp salt
- ½ tsp freshly ground black pepper
- ½ large head red or green cabbage, or a combination, shredded (8 cups)

Instructions:

1. Combine vinegar, mustard, and garlic in a salad bowl.

2. Add oil, whisking until dressing thickens.

3. Stir in parsley, scallions, salt, and pepper.

4. Add cabbage; toss to coat. Refrigerate for about 30 minutes before serving.

133. Wedge Salad with Gorgonzola Dressing

Ingredients:

- 4 romaine lettuce hearts
- 4 slices cooked bacon, crumbled
- 1 cup cherry or grape tomatoes, halved
- 2 cup beets, roasted or blanched, chilled, diced or cut into wedges
- 1 cup sliced radishes (or cucumber)

Gorgonzola Dressing

- ½ cup full-fat Greek yogurt
- ½ cup mayonnaise
- ¼ cup Gorgonzola, cut into small pieces
- 2 Tbsp lemon juice
- 1 tsp onion powder
- ½ tsp garlic salt
- ¼ tsp freshly ground black pepper
- ¼ tsp sweet paprika

Instructions:

To make the dressing, place the yogurt, mayonnaise, Gorgonzola, lemon juice, onion powder, garlic salt, pepper, and paprika in a medium bowl along with 2 tablespoons warm water and whisk well.

1. Refrigerate until ready to serve.
2. Fill two large bowls with lukewarm water.
3. Add the romaine hearts and soak 3 to 4 minutes while you prepare the dressing.
4. Drain the romaine, wrap in papertowels, and chill in the fridge for at least 1 hour to crisp it up.
5. Cut the romaine hearts in half and place two halves on each plate.
6. Drizzle with the dressing and sprinkle with pepper.
7. Top with the bacon, tomatoes, beets, radishes.
8. Serve with the remaining dressing.

134.   Tomato and Red Onion Salad

Ingredients:

- 3 Tbsp red wine vinegar
- 2 tsp Dijon mustard
- ¾ tsp salt
- ½ tsp freshly ground black pepper
- 5 Tbsp extra-virgin olive oil

- 3 large tomatoes, cut into 1-inch pieces
- ½ small red onion, thinly sliced
- ½ seedless cucumber, cut into ⅓-inch dice
- ¼ cup chopped fresh basil or dill
- 2 Tbsp capers, rinsed and drained

Instructions:

1.Combine first four ingredients in a salad bowl. Add oil, whisking until dressing thickens.

2.Add tomatoes, cucumbers, onion, basil, and capers; toss gently and serve right away.

135. Cream of Mushroom Soup

Ingredients:

- 8 ounces mushroom -- white button, finely chopped
- 1/4 cup chopped onion -- finely chopped
- 2 stalks celery -- finely chopped4 tablespoons butter
- 2 cups heavy cream
- 2 cans chicken stock

- 2 tablespoons flour
- 1 teaspoon salt
- 1/2 teaspoon pepper -- to taste

Directions:

1. In a large saucepan, melt butter over medium heat.
2. Add finely diced veggies and saute, stirring occasionally, for about 5 minutes or until they wilt.
3. Add in the flour and stir well.
4. Let cook, stirring, for about 1 minute, then pour in the chicken stock and cream, whisking constantly.
5. Bring to a simmer and cook about 5 minutes, whisking occasionally.

136.   Easy Chicken Noodle Soup

Ingredients:

- 2 tablespoons butter
- 1/4 onion
- 2 stalks celery
- 5 baby carrots
- 14 1/2 ounces chicken broth -- 1 can

- 10 ounces canned chicken -- 1 can
- Salt and Pepper to taste
- 1 teaspoon Wylers Shaker Instant Bouilion
- Chicken Garlic and Herb flavor or 1 chicken bouillon cube
- 1/2 package shiratake noodles

Directions:

1. Chop onion,celery and carrots. Brown them in the butter for a few min.
2. Add the broth, chicken, noodles and seasoning.
3. Bring to boil and then turn down and simmer for a few min.
4. I can get 4 or 5 good size servings.
5. You can add green bean, zucchini as well.

137.   Ground Beef Soup

Ingredients:

- 1 pound ground beef
- 1 cup diced onion
- 1 diced green bell pepper
- 8 cups beef stock
- 2 cups diced carrots -- i used 1 cup
- 1 cup diced celery
- 2 cups chopped tomatoes
- 1/4 cup minced fresh parsley1 package broccoli, frozen -- cut into
- florets
- or 1 head cut into floretswith stalks
- peeled and diced
- 1 teaspoon dried oregano
- 1 teaspoon dried thyme
- freshly ground black pepper to taste

Directions:

1. In large non-stick skillet, sauté; ground beef over medium heat.

2. Add onions, garlic and bell pepper and continue sautéing until meat is tender and vegetables have softened, about 5 minutes. Drain fat from pan and set meat mixture aside.

3. In large soup pot or Dutch oven, heat beef stock over medium-high heat until boiling.

4. Add carrots and celery and cook until almost tender, about 5 minutes.

5. Add tomatoes, broccoli, parsley, seasonings and reserved meat mixture.

6. Mix well. Simmer over low heat 10 minutes until all vegetables are tender.

7. Taste and adjust seasonings.

138.   Low-carb Chicken Soup

Ingredients:

- 2 leeks -- washed and sliced to 1" slices
- 3 turnips -- peeled, cut in chunks
- 1 bell pepper -- cut in 1" pieces
- 5 celery stalks -- cut in 1" pieces
- 4 chicken breast -- cut in bitesize pieces

- 32 ounces chicken broth -- I used a box variety2 cups water
- 1 clove garlic
- 1/4 teaspoon red pepper flakes
- 1 teaspoon salt
- fresh ground pepper to taste
- 1/2 teaspoon goya adobo seasoning
- 1/4 teaspoon thyme

Directions:

In large pot combine all ingredients and cook on low heat till turnips are tender.

Serves 6 to 8 hearty bowls.

139.   Quick Sausage Soup

Ingredients:

- 1 pound ground pork sausage
- 3 tablespoons butter
- 1 1/2 tablespoons garlic -- crushed
- 1 1/2 tablespoons minced onion1 can beef broth
- 1 cup heavy cream

- 1 can green beans -- drained
- 1 cup carrots -- cooked
- pepper to taste

Directions:

1. Brown ground pork sausage in skillet.
2. In saucepan, melt butter.
3. Add garlic and onions and brown in melted butter.
4. Add sausage and remaining ingredients.
5. Heat thoroughly.

140. Vegetable Soup

Ingredients:

- leftover roast beef - shredded or cut up - add au jus and water
- 1/2 medium onion -- cut up
- 1/2 green pepper -- cut up
- 4 medium mushrooms -- cut up
- 1 clove garlic -- chopped fine
- 1/2 head cauliflower -- cut in florets
- 1/2 cup celery -- finely chopped
- salt and pepper -- to taste
- cajun seasoning -- to taste

Directions:

Simmer all ingredients in soup pot for several hours. Eat Hardy!!!

141.   Hearty Beef Stew

Ingredients:

- 1 1/2 pounds beef stew meat
- 14 1/2 ounces stewed tomatoes (1 can)
- 14 1/2 ounces beef broth (1 can)
- 1 cube beef bouillon
- 1/2 teaspoon onion powder

- 1/4 teaspoon garlic powder1 teaspoon salt
- 1/4 teaspoon pepper
- 1/4 teaspoon thyme
- 1 large rutabaga -- (or two small turnips)
- 2 medium zucchini

Directions:

1. Brown stew beef in olive oil on all sides in medium high pot. Add tomatoes, broth, spices and water to cover beef.
2. Turn heat down and simmer for about 1 and 1/2 hours.
3. Add cubed (about 1 inch) rutabagas and simmer for 30 minutes.
4. Add diced zucchini and simmer for 30 more minutes.
5. Add more liquid if necessary (to cover the veggies).
6. Taste for seasonings.

142. Chocolate Chip Cookies

Ingredients:

- Olive oil spray
- ½ cup coconut oil, at room temperature
- 2 large eggs
- 1 tsp vanilla extract
- ½ tsp almond extract (optional)

- 1½ cups almond flour
- ¼ cup stevia
- ½ tsp baking soda
- 1 tsp ground cinnamon
- ¼ tsp salt
- ½ cup sugar-free chocolate chips

Instructions:

1. Preheat the oven to 375°F.
2. Coat a baking sheet with olive oil spray.
3. Place next four ingredients in a bowl, and beat with a hand mixer for about 1 minute.
4. Mix together the remaining ingredients (except chocolate chips).
5. Beat the almond flour mixture into the wet ingredients until the dough comes together.
6. Drop the cookie dough onto the prepared baking sheet by teaspoonfuls.
7. Gently flatten the cookies by pressing with a fork or spatula.
8. Top each cookie with chocolate chips. Bake 10 minutes, until lightly browned.
9. Let cool completely before serving.

143. Chocolate-Orange Soufflés

Ingredients:

- 5 Tbsp butter, plus more for ramekins
- ⅓ cup granular sugar substitute, plus more for ramekins
- 6½ ounces low-carb or sugar-free chocolate bars
- 1 tsp orange extract
- 5 large eggs, separated
- ¼ tsp cream of tartar

Instructions:

1.Heat oven to 425°F. Lightly butter 6 ramekins; coat the insides with sugar substitute. Set on a baking sheet.

2.Melt chocolate, butter, and orange extract in a small saucepan over low heat. Transfer to a medium bowl. Whisk in egg yolks; set aside.

3.Add egg whites and cream of tartar into another medium bowl; whip with an electric mixer on high speed until frothy. Slowly add sugar substitute; whip until soft peaks form, about 3 minutes. Add one-third of the egg whites into chocolate mixture; gently fold in remaining whites. Divide batter among ramekins; bake until puffed and set, about 13 minutes. Serve right away.

144. Lickety-Split Vanilla Ice Cream

Ingredients:

- 3¼ cups heavy cream
- ½ cup plus 1 Tbsp granular sugar substitute
- Pinch salt
- ½ tsp pure vanilla extract

Instructions:

1.Combine cream, sugar substitute, salt, and vanilla in a medium bowl and refrigerate until very well chilled, at least 1 hour.

2.Process according to the instructions for your ice cream maker.

3.Transfer to a container and freeze until ready to serve. Scoop into dessert dishes.

145.   Coconut Cookies

Ingredients

- 1/3 cup dried coconut
- 5 tablespoons unsweetened coconut milk
- 1 tablespoon vanilla extract
- 1 tablespoon coconut extract (optional)
- ½ teaspoon salt
- ½ cup unsweetened shredded coconut
- 1 cup almond flour or whole grain soy flour

Directions:

1. In a large mixing bowl, whisk the coconut milk, vanilla, coconut extract and salt until the mixture reaches a smooth consistency.
2. Stir in the almond flour or soy flour and the dried coconut.
3. For best results, cover the dough and let it chill in the fridge for 5 minutes.
4. Using a spoon, scoop the dough and drop onto a baking sheet that's been sprayed with cooking spray.
5. Make sure each scoop is about one tablespoon in size.
6. The balls should be 1 or 2 inches apart.
7. Bake the cookies for 14 to 20 minutes or until golden brown.

8. Allow the cookies to cool on a tray before serving.

9. Store in parchment paper for up to 5 days in the fridge.

146. Berries and Cream

Ingredients

- 1/2 cup raspberries
- 1/2 cup blueberries
- 1/3 cup heavy cream or Greek yogurt (unsweetened)
- 1 tablespoon vanilla extract
- 1 teaspoon lemon zest (optional)
- 1 teaspoon cinnamon (optional)
- 1 teaspoon almonds or crushed nuts (optional)

Directions:

1. Thoroughly rinse the fresh berries and pat dry. You can also use frozen berries or a mixture of fresh and frozen.

2. Depending on your preference and what you have on hand, you can use heavy cream, Greek yogurt or coconut cream as the base to go with the fruit.

3. You can even use combinations, just be mindful of carb intake.

4. In a medium bowl, whip together the heavy cream with the vanilla extract and add in any other flavors you'd like, such as lemon zest or cinnamon.

5. In a small bowl, ramekin, dessert cup or martini glass (depending on how fancy you want to be), drop in the cream mixture and top with the fresh berries.

6. If you'd like you can also use strawberries, sliced peaches, pomegranate seeds or any other fruit and berries that are in season.

147. Bittersweet Chocolate Frosted Brownies

Ingredients

For the brownies:

- 4 ounces of unsweetened baking chocolate
- ½ cup heavy cream
- 5 large eggs
- ½ cup unsalted butter
- 1 tablespoon sugar free vanilla extract
- 1 cup sugar substitute
- 1 ¼ cups wheat bran or oat bran
- 2 teaspoons baking powder
- ½ cup your choice of nuts (optional)

For the frosting:

- ½ cup dark chocolate chips
- 2 tablespoons whole milk
- 2 tablespoons full fat vanilla Greek yogurt (no sugar added)

Directions:

1. Microwave the chocolate together with the butter in a microwave-safe bowl for about 2 minutes (don't leave it going any longer than that without checking).
2. Once the chocolate is fully melted, mix in the heavy cream. In another bowl, beat together the eggs with the sugar substitute using an electric mixer.
3. As you're mixing, add in the vanilla extract.
4. Finally, mix in the wheat or oat bran, nuts and baking powder.
5. Preheat your oven to 325 degrees Fahrenheit.
6. Get out an 8 by 8 inch baking pan and spray it with a butter-based cooking spray.
7. Evenly spread the batter into the pan. Bake the brownies until you can insert a toothpick that comes out clean about 30 to 40 minutes.
8. Remove from the oven and allow to cool.
9. Mix together all the frosting ingredients until well combined.
10. Spread onto the cooled brownies and cut the brownies into bite-sized squares.
11. This recipe makes about 25 brownies.

148. Choco-Mint Mousse

Ingredients:

- 1 ½ cups heavy cream
- 3 scoops of chocolate whey protein powder
- ½ tsp. mint extract

Directions:

1. Pour cream into an electric mixer and beat until thick.

2. Add protein mix and mint extract. Continue to beat until it turns smooth and firm.

3. Chill for 30 minutes and serve.

149.   Decadent Chocolate Cake

Ingredients:

- 4 oz. baking chocolate (unsweetened)
- 8 tbsp. butter (unsalted)
- 2 tbsp. water
- ¾ cup sucralose (granular sugar substitute)
- 2 tbsp. cocoa powder (unsweetened)
- 1 tsp. vanilla extract
- 6 large eggs

Directions:

1. Preheat oven to 325°F. Take an 8-in. spring form baking pan and grease it. Line with parchment paper, grease it, and set aside.

2. Set a double boiler over simmering water and melt chocolate, butter and water in it. Stir occasionally to combine chocolate mixture well. Once it has melted, immediately remove from heat and transfer it to a large bowl. Let it cool to room temperature.

3. Add ¼ cup of the sucralose, the cocoa powder and vanilla extract. Stir well until combined thoroughly.

4. Place eggs in a separate medium bowl. Beat with an electric mixer set on medium-high for about 6 minutes, until thick

ribbons form when the beater is lifted. Reduce the beater's speed to medium and gradually add remaining sucralose while continuously beating eggs for another minute until combined.

5. Take 1/3 of the egg mixture and stir it into the chocolate mixture.

6. Fold in another 1/3 of the egg mixture until well combined, and do the same for the remaining 1/3 egg mixture.

7. Pour the batter into the baking pan. Smoothen the top then place into the oven. Let it bake for 40 to 45 minutes, until it looks like a brownie, with the cake evenly risen and almost set.

8. Let it cool completely on a wire rack. Run a knife around the edges of the pan and place the cake on a platter. Remove the rim and cut into 12 slices. Serve with whipped cream, if desired.

150. Ginger Flan

Ingredients:

- 1 ½ cup heavy cream
- 3 large egg yolks
- 2 large eggs
- 1 cup water
- 8 packets sucralose
- 1 tbsp. fresh ginger
- 1 tsp. vanilla extract

Directions:

1. Preheat oven to 350°F. Fill a roasting pan halfway with boiling water and place in the oven's center shelf.

2. Pulse all the ingredients in a blender until mixture turns very smooth.

3. Pour mixture through a sieve and into a shallow, 1-quart baking dish. Place the dish in the roasting pan. Bake for 30 to 35 minutes.

4. Let flan cool on a wire rack until it reaches room temperature. Spray a plastic wrap with cooking spray and place it over the flan. Let it chill in the refrigerator for 3 hours.

5. Remove plastic wrap, place a large platter over the pan. Turn it over and remove the pan so the flan is on the plate. Divide into 6 servings.

151. Hazelnut Eggnog

Ingredients:

- 6 large eggs
- 1 tsp. sucralose
- 2 cups water
- 1 ½ cups heavy cream
- ½ cup hazelnut syrup (sugar-free)
- 1 tsp. vanilla extract

Directions:

1.Beat eggs and sucralose in a large saucepan.

2.Mix the water, cream and syrup in a bowl. Stir in 2 cups of the mixture into the saucepan. Cook over low heat with constant stirring. Once mixture turns thick enough (can coat a metal spoon), remove from heat and stir in the remaining mixture.

3.Add the vanilla extract and stir well.

4.Cover the saucepan and place it in the refrigerator for at least 3 hours, or overnight. Serve chilled.

152. Cranberry-Orange Fool

Ingredients:

- 1 cup fresh or frozen cranberries
- ⅓ cup water
- 2 tsp freshly grated orange zest
- 1 cup heavy cream, chilled
- 2 Tbsp granular sugar substitute
- ½ tsp pure vanilla extract

Instructions:

1.Simmer cranberries and water over medium-high heat until mixture thickens and cranberries pop, 5–10 minutes. Transfer to a food processor or blender and purée. Pour into a medium bowl. Add orange zest and stir to blend.

2.Meanwhile, whip cream, sugar substitute, and vanilla with an electric mixer on medium-high speed until soft peaks form.

3.Fold one-third of the whipped cream into cranberries; fold in remaining cream. Scoop into dessert bowls and serve, or refrigerate for up to 4 hours.

153. Mini-Muffin-Tin Chocolate Brownies

Ingredients:

-
- 4 Tbsp (½ stick) butter, plus more for muffin tin
- 8½ ounces sugar-free or low-carb dark chocolate
- 3 large eggs
- ⅛ tsp salt
- 1 Tbsp flour

Instructions:

1.Heat oven to 375°F. Lightly butter two 12-cup mini-muffin tins; set aside.

2.Melt butter and chocolate over low heat; let cool slightly.

3.Beat eggs and salt with an electric mixer on high speed. Add flour; beat on low speed just to combine. Add cooled chocolate; whisk on low speed to combine.

4.Divide batter among muffin cups (it will not fill them). Bake until tops are puffed and cracked, about 8–10 minutes. Cool in tin for 5 minutes; transfer to a wire rack to cool completely, about 20 minutes. Serve.

154. Vanilla Meringues

Ingredients:

- 3 large egg whites
- 1-½ tsp clear or regular vanilla extract
- ¼ tsp cream of tartar
- Salt, to taste
- ⅔ cup sugar substitute

Instructions:

1. Heat oven to 200°F. Line two baking sheets with parchment paper; set aside.

2. Combine egg whites, sugar substitute, vanilla and salt in a large bowl; beat with an electric mixer until medium peaks form.

3. Dollop generous tablespoonfuls of meringue onto baking sheets; bake until dry and crisp, about 1 hour.

4. Cool completely on the baking sheet. Serve.

155. Low Carb Jello/Mousse

Ingredients:

- 1 Envleope Unflavored Gelatine
- 1/4 Cup of Splenda
- 1/4 SF Cup of Vanilla Syrup
- 8 Ounce Cream Cheese
- One Small Box of SF Lime Jello One Small Box of SF Strawberry Jello

Directions:

1. First make up your lime jello and start cooling in the fridge.
2. In another bowl mix your cream cheese, splenda & vanilla syrup.

3. In a saucepan boil your water and add non flavored gelatine.
4. Pour the non flavored gelatine into your cream cheese mixture ... mix well and pour all of these ingredients into your lime jello.
5. Let cool in refridgerator for at least 2 hours.
6. Then make your strawberry jello

156.   Easy Chocolate Mousse

Ingredients:

- 1 package sugar free chocolate pudding mix
- 1 pint HEAVY whipping cream

Directions:

1. Get a large metal mixing bowl and fill it with one layer of ice

2. Put a 2nd smaller metal mixing bowl in in the ice bowl and let it get super cold

3. Put pudding mix in smaller bowl, and slowly add whipping cream to it, beating with an electric mixer until its all added in.

4. The longer you mix it, the smoother it becomes.

5. I have done it with super-cold whipping cream and a refrigerated mixing bowl and it works, but for the best effect use the ice bowl method.

6. Portion it into small tea cups or whatever (it should make 6-8 servings) and top with a dollop of sugar-free cool whip if you want, just before eating.

157. Chocolate Macadamia Nut Cheesecake

Ingredients:

- 1 8 oz pk cream cheese
- 1 egg
- 1 cup sour cream
- 1/3 cup (each)of
- 3 artifical sweetners.
- 1/2 cup macadamia nuts unsalted
- 4 ozs. pre-melted unsweetned chocolate.
- Pam spray.

Directions:

1. Cream cheese needs to be softened (set out about 2 hrs).
2. Add sour cream, sweetners, egg and pre-melted chocolate in medium bowl and blend with hand mixer.
3. Add softned cream cheese.
4. Blend well.
5. Add nuts.
6. Pour into pie pan that has been sprayed with Pam spray.
7. Cook in 325 degree oven for 1/2 hr.
8. Turn off the oven and let set in oven for 45 mins.
9. Take out and cool in refrigerator.

158. Gellair

Ingredients:

- 4 oz cream cheese room temperature
- 2 packets of sugar free, flavored gelatin
- 2 cups boiling water 6 ice cubes
- 2 packets sweetener (optional)

Directions:

1. Mix gelatin into boiling water until dissolved.
2. Add ice cubes to gelatin and stir to dissolve.
3. Place mixture in freezer until gelatin is semi-set
4. Mix sweetener into cream cheese or simply stir cheese until smooth if no sweetener is used.
5. You may want to warm cheese in microwave but be careful not to start cooking it.
6. Remove gelatin from freezer and whip with mixer on high until frothy.
7. Gelatin should be set enough to hold air bubbles you're introducing.
8. Add cream cheese and continue to whip until fully blended. Place in refrigerator until set.
9. Result is an airy, somewhat creamy gel with strong flavouring.

159. Fresh Fruit Ice Cream

Ingredients:

- 1 Cup Frozen Berries
- 1/3-1/2 Cup Cream
- 1/4 Teaspoon Vanilla
- Sweetener (as you like)

Directions:

1. Blend all ingredients in a food processor or blender till smooth.
2. Enjoy!

160. Lemon Icebox

Ingredients:

- 8 oz. cream cheese room temp
- 4 tbs lemon juice
- 2/3 cup Splenda
- 1/2 cup whipped cream

Directions:

3. Combine the cream cheese, lemon juice and splenda.
4. Whip until smooth fold in the whipped cream gently smooth into a pie tin or bowl.
5. Refrigerate for about an hour until firm.
6. Enjoy!

161. Hazelnut Muffins

Ingredients:

- 1 Cup Atkins Bake Mix
- 1/2 Cup Flax Seed Meal
- 1/2 Cup Splenda
- 1 Tsp Cinnamon2 Eggs
- 1/4 Cup of Heavy Cream
- 1/4 Cup of Water
- 1/4 Cup of SF Hazelnut Syrup
- 2 Tblsp. Vegetable Oil

Directions:

1. Combine all dry ingredients in a mixing bowl and stir.
2. Then, add remaining ingredients and blend gently.
3. Spoon into greased muffin pan and bake in preheated oven at 325 for 20 minutes or until golden

162. Death by chocolate

Ingredients:

- 1 box of sugar free instant chocolate pudding
- Cool Whip (as topping, if desired)
- 2 1/2 pints of heavy whipping cream

Directions:

1. Blend the pudding mix with the heavy whipping cream until thick.
2. Separate this dessert into 4 containers and enjoy it throughout the week.

3. Add a big spoonful of Cool Whip to each containerright before eating.

4. This recipe can be made with all sugar free, instant puddings.

5. Butterscotch is my second favorite!

163. Chocolate Ganache

Ingredients:

- 4 oz. Heavy Cream
- 1/2 Cup Sugar Substitute
- 1 Tablespoon Butter
- 2 Teaspoon Vanilla Extract
- 1/4 Cup Cocoa

Directions:

1. Place cream, sugar substitute and cocoa into a meduim saucepan.
2. Place over meduim-high heat and whisk to combine ingredients.
3. Stir constantly for about 3-5 minutes being careful not to burn.
4. Remove from heat and add extract and butter. Stir. Allow to cool.
5. Mixture will thicken as it cool.
6. Mixture will be of a medium fudge consistency when placed in fridge-this makes a great filling for cookies or frosting brownies.

164. Apple Crumble

Ingredients:

Filling

- Olive oil spray
- 1 medium zucchini, peeled and diced
- 1 green apple, cored and diced
- 3 Tbsp stevia
- 1 Tbsp ground cinnamon
- 1 Tbsp wheat bran
- 1 Tbsp coconut oil
- ⅓ cup water

- 1 tsp vanilla extract

Crust

- 1 cup almond flour
- 2 Tbsp stevia
- 2 tsp whole grain soy flour
- ¼ tsp salt
- ¼ cup unsalted butter, chilled, cut into chunks

Instructions:

1.Preheat the oven to 350°F. Coat an 8-by-8-inch pan with olive oil spray. Place the zucchini, apple, stevia, cinnamon, and wheat bran in a medium bowl. Mix well.

2.Heat the coconut oil in a skillet over medium heat. Cook the zucchini-apple mixture, tossing well, 1 to 2 minutes. Reduce the heat to low, pour in the water, and cover. Simmer 6 to 8 minutes, until the apple and zucchini are tender and a thick sauce forms. Set aside.

3.Pulse all the crust ingredients in a food processor until a crumbly dough forms. Press half the crust mixture into the prepared pan. Bake 10 to 15 minutes. Spoon the zucchini-apple mixture over the crust, and sprinkle the remaining crust mixture on top.

165. Mascarpone Parfait

Ingredients:

- 1 cup heavy cream
- 8 oz. mascarpone (softened slightly)
- 1 tbsp. sucralose

Directions:

1. Beat heavy cream to soft peaks with an electric mixer set on medium-high speed.

2. Reduce the speed to medium and gradually add the mascarpone and sucralose while beating mixture continuously for 15 to 30 seconds, until mixture is smooth.

3. Spoon mixture into four parfait cups. Serve garnished with lemon peel or mint sprigs if desired.

166. Double Chocolate Brownies

Ingredients:

- Olive oil spray
- 4 ounces unsweetened chocolate, chopped
- ½ cup unsalted butter
- ¼ cup canned coconut milk
- ½ cup stevia
- ¼ cup almond flour
- 3 Tbsp unsweetened cocoa powder, divided
- 1 tsp baking powder

- 4 large eggs, whisked

Instructions:

1.Preheat the oven to 325°F. Coat an 8-by-8-inch pan with olive oil spray. Place the chocolate, butter, and coconut milk in a bowl and microwave on high power for approximately 2 minutes. Whisk well, and cool for 5 minutes while you prepare the dry ingredients.

2.Place the stevia, almond flour, 2 tablespoons of the cocoa powder, and baking powder in a large bowl, and mix well. Add in the eggs and the cooled chocolate. Transfer to the prepared pan, and smooth the top with a spatula.

Bake for 25 minutes. Let cool, then cut into 18 pieces (three rows of six brownies).

3. Sprinkle with the remaining cocoa powder. Serve.

167. Salted Caramel Cheesecake Bites

Ingredients:

- ½ cup heavy cream
- ⅓ cup plain protein powder
- 2 Tbsp stevia
- 6 ounces full-fat cream cheese, room temperature
- ⅓ cup chopped almonds or macadamia nuts

- 1 Tbsp sugar-free caramel syrup
- 1 tsp vanilla extract
- ⅛ tsp xanthan gum (optional)
- ¼ tsp sea salt or Maldon sea salt flakes

Instructions:

1. Place the heavy cream in a large mixing bowl with the protein powder and stevia.
2. Whisk until smooth.
3. Add the cream cheese, almonds or macadamia nuts, caramel syrup, and vanilla extract, and blend until smooth.
4. Sprinkle the mixture with the xanthan gum, if desired, and mix again for about 30 seconds.
5. The mixture will thicken slightly.
6. Cover a tray that will fit into your freezer with a sheet of wax paper.
7. Use a soup spoon to scoop the mixture onto the tray, make 18 mounds.
8. Alternatively, you can use two silicone candy melds or coat an empty ice cube tray with olive oil spray, and press spoonful of the cheesecake mixture into 18 of the melds.
9. Sprinkle with the sea salt. Freeze at least one hour before serving.

168. Mexican Wedding Cookies

Ingredients:

- 2 cups almond flour
- 1 cup finely chopped walnuts
- ¼ cup whole grain soy flour
- 1 tsp baking powder

- 1 tsp ground cardamom
- ¼ tsp salt
- ¼ cup unsalted butter, softened
- 1 large egg
- 1 tsp vanilla extract
- ½ cup stevia, divided
- 1 Tbsp ground cinnamon

Instructions:

1.Preheat the oven to 325°F, and line two baking sheets with parchment paper.

2.In a bowl, whisk together the almond flour, walnuts, soy flour, baking powder, cardamom, and salt.

3.In another bowl, beat the butter for about 2 minutes. Beat in the egg, vanilla extract, and half the stevia. Then beat in the almond flour mixture until the dough comes together. Form the dough into ¾-inch balls, and place on the baking sheets about 1 inch apart.

4.Bake for about 18 minutes, until just lightly golden brown. In a medium bowl, add the remaining stevia and cinnamon, and mix well. Roll the cookies around in the cinnamon mixture to coat. Transfer to a plate to cool completely. Serve.

169. Mock Strawberry Shortcake

Ingredients:

- 1-2 Boxes SF FF Vanilla Pudding mix
- Frozen, No sugar added whole strawberries
- Heavy whipping cream
- 1 Can of real whipped cream
- 4-5 packets of splenda
- water

Directions:

1. Thaw strawberries.

2. Put in sealable bowl with a little water and Splenda to taste.

3. Shake well to mix water with juice of strawberries. refrigerate for at least 1/2 hour.

4. Empty dry pudding into bowl. slowly add whipping cream while beating with electric mixer. Keep adding until pudding is the consistency of thick custard. Refrigerate until ready to use.

5. Add some pudding/custard in bowl and top with strawberries.

6. Top straberries with whipped cream and spoon a little juice from strawberries over whole dessert.

170.   Pumpkin roll Serves

Ingredients:

- 3 eggs
- 2 packets sweetnlow
- 2/3 cup pumpkin
- 1/2 t. ginger
- 1T. cinnamon
- 1T. baking powder
- 1T. baking sodaFilling:
- 4 oz. cream cheese
- 2T. butter
- 2 packets sweetnlow
- 1t. vanilla
- 1T. heavy cream

Directions:

1. Bake for 15 minutes at 350.
2. Beat eggs for 5 minutes.
3. Add remaining ingredients and mix. Spread onto a well greased sided cookie sheet.
4. The layer of batter will be very thin.
5. Remove and let cool.

6. Turn out on a couple of paper towels doubled. (I used an egg turner to loosen from the pan)Roll up in the paper towels.

7. Lay aside. Beat cream cheese and butter until smooth. Add remaining ingredients and beat until blended. Unroll the log and spread on the filling.

8. Roll back up without the paper towels.

9. Refrigerate for at least a half an hour.

10. Start at the end and cut into app. 1/2 " sections as much as you want at that particular time.

11. Will look like a pinwheel.

12. Vary by adding adding pecans. (sprinkle over batter before baking).

171.   Creamy Nutty Gelatin

Ingredients:

- 2 packages of Sugar-Free Gelatin (I used Strawberry-Banana)
- 3 Cups Water
- 1 Cup Heavy Cream
- 1 Cup Nuts (I used Walnuts - but you can substitute your favorite)

Directions:

1. Prepare gelatine as instructed on package, substituting 1 cup of water for 1 cup of cream.
2. Add nuts and chill.
3. For an extra treat, try whipping some cream and adding a dollop on top.

172. Chocoholic Fix

Ingredients:

- 1 chocolate Endulge bar
- 2 tablespoons Kroger nut
- topping Kroger brand whipped cream in a can
- two tablespoons, or as much as you can afford in carbs.

Directions:

1. Break Endulge bar into a custard cup, microwave until melted.
2. Blend nut topping into melted chocolate and top with whipped cream.

173. Chocolate Mousse

Ingredients:

1 envelope unflavoured gelatin

2 tablespoons unsweetened cocoa

2 eggs, separated 2 cups half & half divided

5 packets sugar substitute 1 1/2 teaspoons vanilla

Directions:

1. In medium-size saucepan, mix gelatine and cocoa.
2. In separate bowl, beat egg yolks with 1 cup half-half.
3. Blend into gelatine mixture. Let stand 1 minute to soften gelatine. Stir over low heat until gelatine is completely dissolved, about 5 minutes.
4. Add remaining half-half, sweetener and vanilla.
5. Pour into large bowl and chill, stirring occasionally, until mixture mounds slightly when dropped from spoon.
6. In separate large bowl, beat egg whites until soft peaks form; gradually add gelatine mixture and beat until doubled in volume, about 5 minutes.
7. Chill until mixture is slightly thickened.
8. Turn into dessert dishes or 1-quart bowl and chill until set.

174. Basic Ice Cream Custard

Ingredients:

- 6 ½-cup servings
- 2 cups heavy cream
- 4 egg yolks
- ½ vanilla bean, slit open and scraped
- 8 packets sugar substitute

Directions:

1. Heat cream in a heavy sauce pan over a low heat. Whisk in one egg yolk at a time.
2. Add vanilla bean scrapings and whisk until custard begins to thicken.
3. Remove from heat and cool.
4. Beat one packet of sugar substitute at a time into cooled custard. At this point the custard is ready to add recipe ingredients that make it ice cream (see recipes that follow).
5. Do not overlook the value of refrigerating the custard as it is and using it as a delicious, rich dessert.
6. Or you could whisk in a tablespoon of brandy or brandy flavoring and serve it over berries.

175. Raspberry Sorbet

Ingredients:

- 8 ½-cup servings
- 1 cup heavy cream
- 2 egg yolks
- 1 teaspoon lemon extract
- 8 packets sugar substitute
- 1 cup raspberries
- ½ cup No-Cal raspberry syrup
- ½ cup Framboise (red raspberry liqueur)

Directions:

1. Heat cream on low heat.
2. Whisk in egg yolks one at a time. Add lemon extract and 4 packets of sugar substitute.
3. Whisk until mixture begins to thicken.
4. Remove from heat. Wash and dry raspberries. Place in a bowl.
5. Sprinkle with 4 packets of sugar substitute. Add raspberry syrup and Framboise.
6. Mix well.
7. Whisk raspberry mixture into cream mixture. Cool to room temperature.
8. Place mixture in ice cream maker and churn according to manufacturer's directions.

176.   Chocolate Peanut Butter Cookies

Ingredients:

- 24 cookies
- ¾ cup soy flour
- 2 teaspoons cocoa
- 1½ teaspoons baking powder
- 4 packets sugar substitute

- pinch salt
- ⅓ cup peanut butter
- 1 egg, beaten
- 1 teaspoon melted butter
- ½ cup heavy cream
- 1 teaspoon vanilla extract
- ½ teaspoon chocolate extract

Directions:

1. Preheat oven to 375° F.
2. Sift dry ingredients into bowl.
3. Combine peanut butter with remaining ingredients and add to flour mixture.
4. Stir until blended.
5. Drop by teaspoon onto greased cookie sheet. Bake for 10–12 minutes until brown.

177.   Lemon Sponge Cake

Ingredients:

- ½ cup heavy cream
- 1 cup soy flour
- 1½ teaspoons baking powder
- dash salt
- 3 eggs
- 8 packets sugar substitute
- 2 teaspoons vanilla extract

Directions:

1. 1 teaspoon lemon extract
2. Preheat oven to 300° F.
3. Scald cream and remove from heat.
4. Sift flour, baking powder, and salt together.
5. Beat eggs and sugar substitute thoroughly until thick and lemon colored.
6. Blend in flour mixture just until smooth.
7. Add warm cream and extracts to mixture.
8. Pour batter immediately into a 9-inch greased tube pan.

Bake for 45 minutes, or until done.

178. Marzipan

Ingredients:

- 24 1-inch forms
- 17-ounce package unsweetened grated coconut
- 1 package diet gelatin (any fruit flavor)
- 1 cup ground almonds
- ½ cup heavy cream
- 4 packets sugar substitute
- ½ teaspoon vanilla extract
- ½ teaspoon almond extract

Directions:

1. Combine all ingredients.
2. Shape into any designs you like—fruits, vegetables, and so forth. (Food coloring may be added to simulate true details.)

Chill until forms hold their shape.

179. Almond Pie Crust

Ingredients:

- 1 pie crust
- 1 cup soy flour
- ½ cup ground almonds
- 2 packets sugar substitute
- pinch cinnamon
- ⅓ cup butter, chilled

Directions:

Preheat oven to 400° F.

1. Stir first 4 ingredients together. Cut in butter. Work well into dry ingredients.
2. Cover with wax paper and refrigerate for 1 hour.
3. Place in pie pan patting crumb mixture over sides and bottom with back of spoon.
4. Use fork tines to decorate edges of pie crust and to prick holes in bottom and sides of crust.
5. Place empty disposable pie plate over pie (to keep crust from puffing).
6. Bake for 30 minutes until solid and brown around edges.

7. Remove second pan, cover edges with foil, and allow center to brown thoroughly (about 5 minutes).
8. Cool.

180. Coffee Cream Layer Cake

Ingredients:

- 5 egg whites, at room temperature
- 6 packets sugar substitute
- 2 cups heavy cream
- 1½ teaspoons instant decaffeinated coffee
- ½ tablespoon gelatin
- 1 tablespoon cold water

- 3 tablespoons butter, at room temperature
- 4 egg yolks at room temperature
- 2 teaspoons mocha extract
- ½ cup chopped walnuts

Directions:

1. Preheat oven to 275° F.
1. Butter 3 round layer cake pans.
2. Beat egg whites until they form soft peaks. Add 1 packet sugar substitute and beat until stiff. Divide whites among 3 pans. Bake for 45 minutes.
3. Combine 1 cup heavy cream and instant decaf coffee in top of double boiler.
4. Stir with wire whisk until powder dissolves. Dissolve gelatin in cold water.
5. Add gelatin to coffee mixture and heat just to boiling. Stir constantly with whisk.
6. Remove from heat. Beat in 4 egg yolks, 1 yolk at a time. Add butter and beat well until dissolved.
7. Add extract and remaining sugar substitute. Put in freezer to cool.
8. Whip remaining cup heavy cream until stiff.
9. When coffee mixture is cool, fold into whipped cream and refrigerate until layers are cooked and cooled. Pile cream between layers of meringue as you would frost a layer cake.
10. Top with cream, making sure to cover sides.

11. Sprinkle nuts on top and sides. Refrigerate until serving time.

181.   Pumpkin Chiffon

Ingredients:

- 1 envelope unfavored gelatin
- ½ teaspoon salt
- ½ teaspoon nutmeg
- ½ teaspoon cinnamon
- ¼ teaspoon ginger
- ½ cup cold water
- 2 egg yolks, slightly beaten
- 1 cup heavy cream
- 1¼ cups canned pumpkin
- 8 packets sugar substitute
- 2 egg whites

Directions:

1. Combine gelatine, salt, and spices.
2. Add ¼ cup water. Stir. Mix egg yolks with heavy cream, ¼ cup water, and pumpkin in top of double boiler. Add gelatine mixture.
3. Cook over boiling water for 10 minutes, stirring constantly.
4. Refrigerate until thick as unbeaten egg whites. Stir occasionally.

5. Add sugar substitute (taste for sweetness).

6. Beat egg whites until stiff. Fold chilled pumpkin mixture into egg whites.

7. Be careful not to break down volume of egg whites.

8. Turn into 1½-quart soufflé dish.

9. Refrigerate.

CPSIA information can be obtained
at www.ICGtesting.com
Printed in the USA
LVHW060050210621
690567LV00028B/980

9 781801 884990